William Gass

Twayne's United States Authors Series

Frank Day, Editor

Clemson University

TUSAS 564

William Gass
Photograph courtesy of Herb Weitman, Washington University in St. Louis.

William Gass

By Watson L. Holloway

Brunswick College

Twayne Publishers
A Division of G. K. Hall & Co. • *Boston*

William Gass
Watson L. Holloway

Copyright 1990 by G. K. Hall & Co.
All rights reserved.
Published by Twayne Publishers
A division of G. K. Hall & Co.
70 Lincoln Street
Boston, Massachusetts 02111

Copyediting supervised by Barbara Sutton.
Book production by Janet Z. Reynolds.
Book design by Barbara Anderson.
Typeset in 11 pt. Garamond by Compositors Corporation, Cedar Rapids, Iowa.

First published 1990.
10 9 8 7 6 5 4 3 2 1

Library of Congress Cataloging-in-Publication Data

Holloway, Watson L.
    William Gass / by Watson L. Holloway.
       p.   c.m. — (Twayne's United States authors series ; TUSAS 564)
    Includes bibliographical references.
    ISBN 0-8057-7605-2
    1. Gass, William H., 1924-   — Criticism and interpretation.
  I. Title. II. Series.
PS3557.A845Z68   1990
813'.54—dc20   89-71696
                                             CIP

Dedicated to my parents, George and Sara,
and to my aunts, Mary and Florrie

Contents

About the Author

Watson L. Holloway is an associate professor of English and chairman of the Division of General Studies (Arts and Sciences) at Brunswick College, Brunswick, Georgia. He received his B.A. from the University of California at Los Angeles, his M.A. from the University of Southern California, and his Ph.D. from Emory University. He has published articles on modern British and American writers, including David Jones and John Fowles. He has also published and lectured in the fields of technical writing and educational administration. At present he is at work on a novel.

In addition to his academic work, Watson Holloway has served as a secondary school administrator, a college dean of students, and an intercollegiate coach. He lives in the coastal region of Georgia with his wife, Jane, and his children, Ian, David, Noel, Shane, and Sarah.

Preface

William Gass is what I would call an emerging figure in contemporary literature. I prefer this category because, on the one hand, despite many years of comparatively slight book sales, he continues to be talked about among critics and in academia. On the other hand, he has no mass appeal, and has never courted readers of best-sellers. Despite substantial and enduring critical approval of his novel, his collection of stories, and his two books of critical essays, William Gass has remained a "difficult" writer, one who is read and appreciated almost exclusively in academia. For this reason, Gass cannot be said yet to have left the ranks of the obscure. In the world of the school, however, and in the serious literary circles that interact with that world, the reputation of William Gass has steadily gained ground over the years. Numerous scholarly articles and a book on Gass have appeared recently, accelerating his "emergence" into a lasting literary reputation.

Literary criticism thrives on the coining of new labels for the latest phenomena in fiction; finding a name for Gass and many of his avant-garde contemporaries, however, has been difficult. Several denominations have become associated with the kind of fiction that Gass writes: postmodernist, antirealist, surfictionist, metafictionist, and an old one that Gass himself prefers— modernist. All the above are useful in discussing the work of William Gass because his writing is multidimensional; it grows in one direction without leaving everything else behind. It doubles back on itself, but it also spirals ahead. It is both modernist and postmodernist, metafictional and referential. There is both the experimentalist and the realist about him. Like his friend Stanley Elkin Gass is, to throw in yet another label, a "middle grounder."[1]

This middle position between polarities is not easily won, however; Gass seems always to write against an extreme, an opposite, stretching characters between dialectical boundaries, walling in metaphors and points of view that even in the depths of their aesthetic, rhetorical isolation point steadily to the world outside themselves and long to make contact with that world. The Reverend Jethro Furber in *Omensetter's Luck* is perpetually at odds with his Brackett Omensetter, hating and loving his antagonist. Such is the paradigm for the fiction of William Gass.

Although it is tempting to frame Gass neatly in the box of sixties experimentalism and radical, antirealist self-indulgence, I cannot but see in the extravagant metafictionist the ghost of his opposite. I hope in the following pages to call out that specter of traditionalism (as practiced by Saul Bellow, John Updike, Joan Didion, Ann Beattie, Marilyn Robison, Raymond Carver, and so on) that moves behind the ornate curtain of self-referential artifice (Ronald Sukenick, Raymond Federman, Steve Katz), and that, in its dialectical tension with its other limit, produces a "midfiction" like that of Stanley Elkin, Max Apple, Donald Barthelme, Thomas Pynchon, Don DeLillo, Robert Coover, John Irving (perhaps even the "greats" of the classic novel such as Cervantes, Sterne, and Joyce).[2]

If a glimpse of the world occasionally "emerges" from Gass's finely tuned word machine, it is still the language that must be at the root of any appreciation of his work. For this reason, I engage in a fairly close reading, paying greater attention to the formal qualities of the text than is customary in an introductory study. To understand Gass is first to catch the music and the structural intricacy of his work.

Watson L. Holloway

Brunswick College

Acknowledgments

I am grateful to Alfred A. Knopf for permission to quote from *The World within the Word;* to the Board of Trustees of the University of Illinois and the University of Illinois Press for permission to quote from *Anything Can Happen: Interviews with Contemporary American Novelists;* to Southern Illinois University Press for permission to quote from *The Fiction of William Gass;* and to *Shenandoah* for permission to quote from "A Symposium on Fiction: Donald Barthelme, William Gass, Grace Paley, Walker Percy" (27, no. 2 [Winter 1976]). I am also grateful for permission to quote from *Omensetter's Luck* by William H. Gass. © 1966 by William H. Gass. Reprinted by arrangement with New American Library, a division of Penguin Books USA, Inc. I also wish to thank Herb Weitman of Washington University in St. Louis for permission to use his photograph of William Gass. Finally, I express my appreciation to the library staff of Brunswick College, especially to Virginia Boyd, for their assistance in research, and to Jackie Taylor, Pam Mathis, and Lynette Murphy for their patience and excellent secretarial skills.

Chronology

1924   William Howard Gass born 30 July to William Bernard and Claire Sorensen Gass in Fargo, North Dakota.

1947   Receives A.B. in philosophy from Kenyon College.

1950   Begins teaching at the College of Wooster in Ohio.

1950   Writes some short stories; begins writing *Omensetter's Luck*.

1952   Marries Mary Patricia O'Kelley, with whom he will have three children: Richard, Robert, and Susan.

1954   Receives Ph.D. in philosophy from Cornell University.

1955   Becomes an assistant professor of philosophy at Purdue University.

1958–1959   Serves as visiting lecturer in English and philosophy at the University of Illinois.

1966   Spends a year in England. *Omensetter's Luck* published.

1966   Receives Rockefeller Foundation grant.

1968   *Willie Masters' Lonesome Wife* published.

1969   Becomes a professor of philosophy at Washington University.

1969   Marries Mary Alice Henderson, with whom he has twin children: Elizabeth and Catherine.

1969–1970   Receives Guggenheim Foundation grant.

1970   Spends a year in Portugal.

1970   *Fiction and the Figures of Life* published.

1974   Receives D. Litt. from Kenyon College.

1975   Receives National Institute of Arts and Letters Prize in Literature.

1976   *On Being Blue* published.

1978   *The World within the Word* published.

1985   *Habitations of the Word* published.

Chapter One

William H. Gass: Of Anger and Style

Diddling Away in Corners

In 1966 two neophyte fiction writers published novels: John Gardner produced a traditional, realist work, *The Resurrection;* William Gass saw his antirealist or metafictional novel, *Omensetter's Luck,* appear in print. Twelve years later the same two authors published books about literary criticism and theory that became well known, talked-about, and perhaps more problematic than their authors' fiction: Gardner wrote *On Moral Fiction* and Gass *The World within the Word.* And in that same year, 1978, the writers met on the campus of the University of Cincinnati to argue their theoretical differences. Even though the two had been engaged for years in a polemical duel in print (and "at parties in kitchens at 3 A.M.," according to Gass[1]), this face-to-face confrontation has come to be thought of as a major skirmish in the perennial verbal war between realists and formalists, between traditionalists and the new school of American avant-garde experimentalists that developed during the 1960s. One critic has called this protracted discussion the "showdown on Mainstreet."[2] Only a segment of the dialogue was recorded and published, but in the available version a fundamental cleavage emerges: fiction conceived as a faithful recalling of day-to-day reality rubs against fiction considered as pure artifice (with no direct links to the objective world).

In this duel, Gardner, the champion of conventional, realist fiction (imaginative writing employed as a "tool" for the exploration of and the understanding of "important matters" in real life), argues for the downplay of language and the writer's technique in favor of letting the reader penetrate the language and arrive at the meat, the message, the communication. Form, in other words, exists mainly for the purpose of helping the author say what needs to be said. Gardner (who died in 1982) believed that life has intrinsic order and that an identifiable good in the human condition can be revealed ("affirmed," is his word[3]) through art. The purpose of the writer's language is

1

to facilitate the reader's appreciation of the same goodness; it is not an end in itself: "always I'm using the tool of language to dig a hole. Other people sometimes use the tool of language to chew on."[4] This view subordinates the writer (the medium at his disposal, his personality, and his craft) to the reader's supposed desire to perceive the world: "the world" defined here as human life in all its complexity, with its beauty, its problems, and its possibilities for improvement. Fiction for Gardner is a moral enterprise, an instrument in society to effect a reaffirmation of humanity. To put it more directly, Gardner's fiction has a job to do; the writer is the worker and language is the machinery to get that job done in the most efficient manner possible.

William Gass, replying to Gardner, does not deny that there are indeed a great number of wrongs to right in the real world. For Gass, however, the realm of fiction is not the proper place for social crusades. The survival of the race does indeed depend on serious confrontation with moral questions. Only if man perdures, maintains Gass, will there be room for artists like himself to "diddle away in corners."[5] He insists that, because all language, and fictional language in particular, "deforms" reality, writing and reading novels cannot be trusted as a means of addressing moral problems. For this purpose, people would find the clarity and precision of thought expressed in mathematics or philosophical logic of greater use. Gass insists that there is really no reliable or practical "truth" *inherent* in fiction. Fiction for him is without functional value; it does not provide an authentic or trustworthy view of things. Writing generates artifacts that are worthwhile in themselves but, in the utilitarian sense, are not necessary. Writers, in Gass's view, spin words into literary webs that are self-consistent and beautiful in their own right; to paraphrase Gass, writers "diddle" in workshops largely isolated from the daily traffic of life.

The Gardner-Gass debate marks off polar boundaries on a very old spectrum. The question of perception and expression has engaged the attention of artists, philosophers, scientists, and mathematicians for millennia. Such speculation most often amounts to a willingness or a refusal to "affirm"—to use again Gardner's word—what can be believed about the world and to employ observational skills and communicative techniques to evaluate it and perhaps make it better; or, realizing that any affirmation of beliefs about the world through fiction is impossible, to glory in the generative system (the fictive process) itself, to withdraw from reality into an intentionally artificial domain and be content with the internal cohesiveness of the artifact alone. In other words (words that recall the heightened anxieties and political passions of midcentury America), the question is: When faced with the raw material of daily life, does the artist choose to be an "activist" challenger or a "sell-out" defender of the status quo? Such polarization, however, suggests a simplicity in matters of fiction (good fiction) that does not really exist. The "problems," whose solution William Gass rules out as not within the province of imaginative literature and whose working out John Gardner saw as the ultimate objective of fiction, nevertheless, could not be ignored. The minds of Americans in the sixties were filled with the momentous issues of the times; naturally, writers had to face up to them. The Gass-Gardner confrontation, therefore, not only places fiction in its familiar dialectic of imagination against world, but it also crystallizes and emblemizes artistic life in the 1960s.

Radicals

The great upheavals of the middle forty years of the twentieth century cut deeply at the roots of life and culture in the United States. The protective foliage of established American society was gouged and in many ways perforated irreparably by the blades of the Great Depression, World War II, the Korean conflict, and especially the war in Vietnam. The unprecedented growth of wealth in the United States spawned a colossal communications and entertainment industry that in turn, with time and the rapid development of affordable electronic instruments, led to an almost unmanageable proliferation of information. Information was broken down into marketable bits; communication in all its forms and fragmentations became a commodity both as knowledge and as diversion.[6]

These factors—war, social upheaval, affluence, and the explosion of information—are commonplace in any description of the 1960s and 1970s; and, of course, a rehearsal of the familiar rhetoric about them usually amounts to a simplistic distortion of their meaning. Nevertheless, mention of these aspects of midcentury American life is called for in an appraisal of the way William Gass and many other Americans began to write literature in what has come to be called the "postmodern" way. Postmodern, or postrealist, fiction was then, and, for the most part, continues to be, "radical." In many ways, American experimental writing is a direct outgrowth of the violence, protest, and discontent of the civil rights movement and Vietnam War era. And although William Gass has rejected labels, particularly that of postmodernist,[7] the sixties resonate strongly in his pronouncements about his work, in his notions about fiction in general, and to a lesser degree, in the work itself.

For William H. Gass and other intellectuals in those days who began making serious aesthetic demands on the art of fiction, the "realist novel," brought to maturity under the molding genius of such writers as Cervantes,

Richardson, Fielding, Hardy, Stendhal, Balzac, and Flaubert, came under attack, as did many other conventional forms of cultural life. Some claimed that the realistic novel had died. In some quarters, at least, its supposed passing away was persistently announced. Writers and critics like John Barth were fond of proclaiming "the death of the novel," and an "exhausted literature."[8] It is probably more accurate to say, however, that for a handful of (mostly academic) writers, readers, and critics, conventional realism in fiction ceased to exert its customary appeal; they believed that conventional fiction writing needed disruption and overhaul. Of course, as everyone knows, for the majority of readers and writers, the traditional form of the novel has lived on quite vigorously.[9] Gardner's view appears to hold true. Even for academic and aesthetically discriminating readers, the realistic novel has persisted, delivering faithfully (if at times idiosyncratically) what most people have expected to find in fiction: linear plots, characters that resemble human beings, language that does not intentionally interfere with the illusions created by its words, and a structure and a tone that stick seriously to the rules of genre.

But the novel has always posed a challenge to convention; according to Alain Robbe-Grillet, the words *new* and *novel* are synonymous, more than merely etymological twins; any true novel departs from what has come before.[10] By the end of the 1960s, however, writers of nontraditional fiction (like Proust, Joyce, and Woolf before them) had begun more aggressively to defy conventions, turning their writing against itself, writing novels and stories about the process of writing novels and stories, exploring and parodying standard forms, and in the process calling close attention to the process of writing fiction. In doing so, a few of these new writers crafted brilliant, exciting, truly innovative works. Since the fiction in this period concerned itself so intensely with the fiction-writing act itself, it has been given new names and a new place in literary history: it has been called "metafiction" (or "surfiction," or "superfiction," or "parafiction"). Realizing the limitations of labels, but at the same time acknowledging the advantages of groupings in a discussion of an author's place in literary history, I prefer to use "metafiction" in relation to William Gass and those who write similar literature. Therefore, the list of metafictionist "diddlers in corners"—Vladimir Nabokov, Joseph Heller, Kurt Vonnegut, Jr., Thomas Pynchon, John Barth, Jerzy Kosinski, Ronald Sukenick, Harry Mathews, Gilbert Sorrentino, Steve Katz, Ishmael Reed, Robert Coover, Stanley Elkin, William Burroughs, Raymond Federman, Donald Barthelme, and many others—includes the name of the most accomplished stylist and aesthetician of this group, William Gass.[11]

A Tame Wild Man

William Howard Gass, born in Fargo, North Dakota, 30 July 1924, was a self-proclaimed "angry man" already in his early forties when he began to write and publish fiction. He has remained angry. Anger, for Gass, is an important ingredient in his work.[12] Although Gass is usually described by interviewers, colleagues, and students as a kindly and affable man, this aggressive side of his temperament blended easily with the revolutionary mentality of the sixties.[13] Unlike most of the young radicals, however, Gass was old enough to have experienced firsthand the two great unsettling shocks of mid-century life: economic depression and war.

Shortly after his birth, his parents, displaced by the Great Depression, moved to Warren, Ohio, where his father was able to find work as a high school teacher. There William Gass spent the days of a childhood that appears to have been tinged with sadness, anger, and frustration. He writes graphically about the rootlessness of those days: "Though I was born in Fargo . . . before I was six months old I had, like Moses, floated away in a woven wicker laundry basket to Ohio where my father had taken a job teaching engineering drawing in the Warren High School. Thus I grew up in a dirty, tense, industrial city, my family moving, as rents and renting went, from house to house—I, from school to school—throughout the Depression."[14] His father suffered from a debilitating form of arthritis; his mother was an alcoholic.[15] Only in the summertime, while the Gass family had a brief reprieve from hard times (when William's father made seasonal money playing semipro baseball in North Dakota where there were many friends and relatives), did life acquire stability. "Even in the dustbowl years," writes Gass, Fargo was "a wide open sunny place where the pace was slow (and consequently quick for children)," and "when the dust was not blowing, summertime seemed heaped up in the sky for miles."[16]

Back in Warren, amid the "smells of oil and metal," young William attempted to escape from the hardships of his family environment through books; he read widely, finding sanctuary in language and ideas. He even wrote an article and sent it to John Crowe Ransom at Kenyon College. But there was really no solace for him at home. He felt that he eventually had to get away from his upbringing entirely, and when he left home for college, he had to close the door on his childhood. Nevertheless, from the time he was seven years old, William Gass, like so many sons who are drawn by some incomprehensible force to follow in the occupational footsteps of their fathers (regardless of how they strive with paternal authority in their adolescence), had thought about a career as a teacher. Despite the aggressiveness, anger, and truculence of his youth, William Gass ironically chose the academic life, the profession of his father. Teaching, he told himself, would afford him the leisure to write, and writing was another enterprise that attracted him from early in his life.[17]

He entered Kenyon College at the beginning of World War II. And like almost all men of his generation, he had his college studies interrupted by military service. What he says about his war duty, however, is not typical. Sounding more like the young activists of the 1960s who attacked military commitment than veterans his own age, Gass relegates his apparently successful stint in the Navy (he left as an officer) to the status of "[playing] sailor for three years."[18] Placing himself in league with the antiwar forces and generally liberal sentiments of the day, he stated the following: "My parents were politically conservative and so, vaguely, was I, but the war woke me up, I began to move left, and recent events have accelerated that move until it is now a hurtle."[19] These sentiments matched those of the campus where he found himself as a professor. The apparent mixing in his mind of war, leftist politics, and opposition to parents, while atypical of World War II veterans, fit quite well with the antimilitary sentiments of the Viet Nam era. Gass thus gives the impression (to me, at least) of having fashioned for himself a kind of hip, activist persona that comes across occasionally in his published interviews and in some of his essays, but luckily did not, to any great degree, find its way into his fiction. The exception to this statement might be the brief glimpses of the younger Gass in his novel-in-progress, "The Tunnel," which Gass himself has said has autobiographical overtones.[20] As far as fiction writing is concerned, Gass would classify himself as fundamentally conservative, although highly innovative and experimental (I discuss this point in chapter 5).

At the end of World War II, Gass returned to Kenyon College to study philosophy, but literature, particularly that with a formalist and symbolist flavor, continued to attract him. He read voraciously, especially the popular innovators of the modernist period, James, Faulkner, and Joyce, among others. These writers, along with the three who would influence his own writing to the greatest degree, Rilke, Valéry, and Stein, reinforced his interest in aesthetics and the philosophy of language.

During his years at Kenyon, Gass audited some courses taught by John Crowe Ransom, a leader of the then predominant school of literary theory known as the New Criticism. New Criticism, which represented a turning away from older literary theory built upon the (once considered inextricable) relationship between a literary work and its author's personality and world, prompted Gass to view fiction as a self-enclosed realm, an entity with its own strong sense of structure, story, and meaning independent in many ways from the life and times of its creator. Although William Gass is very much an avant-gardist in fiction, his aesthetic perspectives still, for the most part, bear the imprint of the New Critics. It is certainly true that in the preface to *In the Heart of the Heart of the Country* Gass, paralleling Jacques Derrida, questions the very idea of a preface, and in the manner of the deconstructionists he posits the notion of intertextuality by insisting that sentences weave webs inside webs. It is also true that *On Being Blue* is replete with word games in true poststructuralist style, and that *Willie Masters' Lonesome Wife* is as fragmented and as idiosyncratic in format and as tricky as Katz's *The Exaggerations of Peter Prince*.[21] But Gass, despite his sustained argument for a radical theory of literature, refuses to ally himself with most postmodernists. In fact, as I have said already, he rejects the label postmodern, preferring to call himself a "purified modernist."[22]

In much of his writing, Gass does not follow the hard-line aesthetic views that he pushes in his debates with Gardner, in his essays, and in his interviews. He sees himself and many of those who have been labeled metafictionists as reworkers of the old tradition rather than as radical iconoclasts like the most extreme experimentalists and the French New Novelists.[23] He sees himself and those peers that he mentions in the above quotation as not new, just "freshly cleaned old hats."[24] His basic allegiance to more accepted notions about literature has kept Gass in the mainstream between the wildest of the innovators on one bank and the slavish perpetuators of the realist status quo on the other. And that is the principal reason for the continuation of interest in the works of William Gass and the growing number of appearances of Gass pieces in anthologies of American literature and in English department syllabi as the century draws to an end.[25]

"A Philosophical Investigation of Metaphor"

In 1947 Gass received his bachelor's degree and entered Cornell University for graduate study in philosophy. These three years were to be formative with regard to his later writing and thinking about literature. His interest in aesthetic theory quickened, and because the Cornell course offerings in aesthetics were scant, he was obliged to change his direction slightly, veering into the study of philosophy of language. He studied with Max Black, a noted authority in symbolic logic and a commentator on the work of Ludwig Wittgenstein, with emphasis on the theory of metaphorical models. Wittgenstein himself came to Cornell to present a series of seminars; William Gass was able to attend these sessions and to interact with this famous theoretician in the field of language and meaning. Echoing a similar statement made by Bertrand Russell, the most famous teacher of Wittgenstein, William Gass called this event "the most important intellectual experience of my life."[26]

Gass's self-consciousness regarding the philosophical process, very much like Wittgenstein's preoccupation with language and Valéry's notions about poetry, is foundational in his writing; but what rescues him from the rhetorical solipsism of some of his cometafictionists, "chewing on the tool of language," as Gardner would say, is his desire for intelligible story at some level. Odyssean "dallying" must yield to forward movement.[27] Gass's doctoral dissertation, "A Philosophical Investigation of Metaphor," reveals the influence of Black and Wittgenstein. He finished it in 1954 during his last year of teaching at the College of Wooster. While at Wooster, he met and married his first wife, Mary Patricia O'Kelley, started a family, "wrote a few short stories, and began the novel *Omensetter's Luck*."[28]

Having received his Ph.D., Gass accepted a teaching position at Purdue University, where he taught for fifteen years. In 1969 he moved to Washington University in St. Louis; he has taught philosophy and literature there ever since. In that same year, Gass married his second wife, Mary Alice Henderson. Tom LeClair visited Gass at the latter's home in St. Louis near the Washington University campus. He describes the writer-philosopher as a "small" and "compact" man who at the time was wearing "cutoffs and a T-shirt," and who reminded LeClair of Nabokov's John Shade from *Pale Fire*. Even seated in an easy chair sipping on a "bottle of Ballantine ale," Gass seemed "combative," his voice "highly inflected and aggressively rhetorical."[29] He, like many of his metafictionist peers, seems to have lived up to his self-imposed label of a "tame wild man."[30]

At Purdue he engaged in some serious fiction writing, writing that he had largely put off until the completion of his graduate studies. These early attempts at fiction grew out of his graduate-school admiration of Gertrude Stein; like Stein, he began experimenting with the basic element of story, the sentence. Writing sentences over and over again produced stories that exhibited a high degree of craftsmanship and polish.[31] *Accent Magazine* accepted most of these early pieces and published a special William Gass issue in the winter of 1958. At the same time, Gass worked away on his first novel, *Omensetter's Luck*, finishing it in 1966. Before Gass could submit the manuscript for publication, however, it was stolen. But the theft proved to be a blessing, because only in the second version did the central and by far the most powerful character, Jethro Furber, appear.[32] After a rewriting, the book, according to Gass, was sent to twelve publishers before it was accepted by New American Library.[33]

This first novel gained immediate recognition as a brilliant piece of writing. Critical applause rang out in some respected places. Richard Gilman in the *New Republic*[34] called *Omensetter's Luck* "the most important work of fiction by an American in this literary generation." *Newsweek*[35] called it "a dense, provoking, vastly rewarding and very beautiful first novel" featuring "prose that rolls along the tongue even in silent reading." That the novel places Gass as a leader of his literary generation is, in my opinion, without question. It is truly, to paraphrase the review in *Newsweek,* dense, seductively lyrical, and intellectually provocative; its future as a lasting work of literary art seems assured.

"To Intrigue, To Dazzle, But Not To Fly"

William Gass's study of the philosophy of language strongly manifests itself in his work, both critical and creative.[36] Like Wittgenstein, Gass insists that the structures of language, and therefore of fiction, have no clear-cut relation to referents but exist instead as entities in their own right, as additions to, not reflections of, the realm of matter.[37] His desire to create a literary "object" with which the reader may comfortably live, one that has a life of its own, places William Gass in a class of writers (many of whom are professional academics like Gass) who are, as Larry McCaffery says, "locked within a world shaped by language and by subjective (i.e., fictional) forms developed to organize our relationship to the world in a coherent fashion."[38]

This is a salient feature of postrealist fiction. For instance, Nabokov, one of the patriarchs of metafiction, allows Kinbote to carve out his Zembla from the text of a poem; Coover's Henry Waugh lives in a paper-and-dice baseball game that he makes up to counter his drab existence as an accountant; Vonnegut's Billy invents his Tralfamador; Pynchon's Oedipa entangles herself in the dark vines of the Tristero conspiracy; and Gass's narrators enclose themselves in small, midwestern towns, in thought-gardens, and behind ice-encrusted windows that all turn out to be idiosyncratic webs of refuge.[39]

Many of these intriguing character portraits in Gass's fiction, language-centers behind walls, appear in his short stories. *In the Heart of the Heart of the Country,* Gass's most talked-about collection of short writing, was published in 1968 and attracted a great deal of critical praise. The book consists of five short pieces, one of them, "The Pedersen Kid," stretching almost to the length of a novella. The characters burrow into themselves and make up aesthetic and ontological systems from their obsessive word flows.

Such fabrications in Gass tend to be circular, open loops, configurations that dance in the mind both during and after reading. William Gass offers a clever analogy as an example of this self-reflective, looping imagery. In *Fiction and the Figures of Life* (a volume of his collected essays that appeared in 1970) he compares his metaphorical textual systems to Renaissance designs of flying machines: "dreams enclosed in finely drawn lines—which are intended to intrigue, to dazzle, but not to fly" (*FFL,* 118). Fiction, in Gass's estimation, is not utilitarian; it is not supposed to do or cause anything in particular. It just *is.* It exists alongside other entities. Like other postrealists, Gass considers futile the attempt to make fiction reflect life. He agrees with Raymond Federman, who maintains that fiction cannot be a mirror, cannot merely reflect a reality exterior to itself. In defiance of conventional expectations, "the shape and order of fiction," writes Federman, "will not result from an imitation of the shape and order of life, but rather from the formal circumvolutions of language as it wells up from the unconscious."[40]

To Gardner's mind, there should be less circumlocution, less transformation of reality and greater rendering of it as it is. The expectation that the author mask his voice, hide his language, make his words so thin that images of the world "as it is" dominate the reader's mind constitutes (for vocal critics like Katz, Sukenick, and Federman) the realist end of the spectrum. At least this is the feature that drew the most fire during the sixties questioning of fictional values, purposes, and techniques. The conventions of the traditional making of novels and stories suddenly seemed to the revolutionary mind staid and insipid. The viewpoints regarding literature, heretofore mixed and syncretistic, reflecting the positioning of almost all writing somewhere along the realist-romanticist scale, thus became suddenly polarized. Many writers and critics, not intrigued or energized by a cold, brutal world of chaos and deception, sought solace from that world in the imagination. Any depiction of an extralinguistic world became suspect; fictional language thus acquired a "thickness," a self-absorption that made the words themselves, rather than what the words could mean, the focus of creative energy. William Gass, like most philosophers who ponder the tenuous tie between language and the world, built his case against realism upon the fact that human beings cannot perceive reality directly—a medium is required.

His novels are recursive, reflexive, metafictional, turning back on themselves, calling attention to themselves as, in Ronald Sukenick's words, "all made up."[41]

This self-absorptive nature of the medium (fictional language) manifests itself in the purpose and content of Gass's quintessential model of metafiction, *Willie Masters' Lonesome Wife*. This short novel, which appeared in *Tri-Quarterly* in 1968, calls attention on every line and on every page to the fact that it is pure invention; that it has absolutely nothing to do with the daily world; that it is "made up" out of words and artwork printed on paper and nothing else; that its language points only to itself and to nothing beyond. Mixing poetry, off-color songs, visual tricks, puzzles, theater, mazes, and a many-leveled narrational structure, Gass creates an outlandish piece of metafiction.

In the way of Jorge Luis Borges and Nabokov, Gass seeks to draw and pull at his audience, and in the process, makes heavy demands upon readers. Even fellow experimentalist Donald Barthelme has taken Gass to task for the latter's hyperselectivity and disdain of the slow-to-follow.[42] And although William Gass has said that he wants only to "fictionalize" the reader, draw him into a two-way metaphor, a model that binds the narrator and the reader as Hardy's sentence "She tamed the wildest flowers" welds subject and object in interactive resonance,[43] the fact remains that he wants his, the writer's, language to dominate the reader. One of Gass's complaints about Barth, Borges, and Beckett is that they allow the reader to remain passive.[44] Grace Paley views this "passivity" that Gass denigrates quite differently: for her it is the need of the reader to have "space to move around," to see what he wants to see even if it is an illusory reality. She chastises him for not providing for "reader creativeness." Gass responds that he does not want to permit the reader to go beyond the limits of the author's language.[45] This apparent contradiction in what Gass wants from the reader offers a point of departure for a consideration of Gass's special place in contemporary literature.

"Against the Grain"

Gass is justified in his objection to the term "postmodern."[46] He is not alone among his generation to find fault with it. John Barth, for instance, considers the denomination "awkward and faintly epigonic, suggestive less of a vigorous or even interesting new direction in the old art of storytelling than of something anti-climactic, feebly following a very hard act to follow."[47] Charles Newman underscores Barth's dislike of the term as suggestive of something at the tail end; he says that "postmodern" brings to

mind "a band of vainglorious contemporary artists following the circus ele-
phants of Modernism with snow shovels."[48] Nevertheless, the term has
stuck in our minds; and it has proved useful. Just as the use of the word
"metafiction" brings together a collection of texts and authors that share elements, so also does the term "postmodernist" provide a convenient juxtaposition of elements that have received various degrees of emphasis from
one literary period to another. In literary evolution, there are certain components that persist; only their interrelationships shift with time. Thus,
even though radicals would like to believe that particular things in literature cease to exist, and that others emerge afresh, in actuality, there is only a
shift of emphasis. At a particular time, some elements dominate; at that
same time others recede. Some features, to slip in some critical jargon, are
"foregrounded," others are "backgrounded." None actually die; none are
freshly born. This notion is put forth clearly in McHale's long summary of
Roman Jakobson's concept of the artistic "dominant." The features that
make up the modernist fictional "dominant," according to McHale, have to
do with knowledge; they are, in effect, questions.[49] Modernism is, in this
view, predominantly epistemological (knowledge-directed). The "exem-
plary modernist text," according to McHale, is Faulkner's *Absalom,
Absalom!,* a detective story, "the epistemological genre *par excellence.*"[50]
Epistemological (modernist) devices in the Faulkner novel (and in the fiction of William Gass) include diverse and juxtaposed perspectives (see particularly *Willie Masters' Lonesome Wife*); evidence focused through a
central "consciousness" (Quentin, Jorge in "The Pedersen Kid," Tott and
Furber in *Omensetter's Luck*); "virtuoso variants on interior monologue"
(Miss Rosa, all of Gass's narrators); and the "typically modernist move":
the transference of "epistemological difficulties" from the characters in the
novel to its reader—the Faulkner novel's "strategies of 'impeded form'
(dislocated chronology, withheld or indirectly-presented information, difficult 'mind styles,' and so on) *simulate* for the reader the very same problems of accessibility, reliability, and limitation of knowledge that plague
Quentin and Shreve."[51] The simulation of epistemological problems for the
reader is a salient feature of Gass's fiction, especially in *Willie Masters',*
"The Tunnel," and in most of the stories in *In the Heart of the Heart of the
Country.* Readers of Gass, forced to sort out sources of information and
puzzle over where that information leads, must exert considerable effort to
get into Gass's world. Epistemological walls abound, giving Gass, along
with Katz, Coover, and Federman, the reputation of difficulty and
inaccessibility.

Crossing the Line

If *Absalom, Absalom!* is a paradigm of modernist fiction, it also contains the seeds of postmodernism. The line is drawn in chapter 8 when Quentin and Shreve find themselves at a dead end in their knowledge of the Sutpen murder; they continue "beyond reconstruction," in McHale's words, "into pure speculation. The signs of the narrative act fall away, and with them all questions of authority and reliability. The text passes from mimesis of the various characters' narrations to unmediated diegesis, from characters 'telling' to the author directly 'showing' us what happened between Sutpen, Henry, and Bon. The murder-mystery is 'solved,' however, not through epistemological processes of weighing evidence and making deductions, but through the imaginative projection of what *could*—and, the text insists, *must*—have happened . . . Quentin and Shreve project a world, apparently unanxiously. Abandoning the intractable problems of attaining to reliable knowledge of *our* world, they improvise a *possible world;* they *fictionalize.*"[52] The text moves at this point from "problems of knowing" to "problems of *modes of being*—from an epistemological dominant to an *ontological one*," says McHale. As Faulkner's text crosses this line dividing epistemological concerns and ontological speculation, from knowledge of the world to the projection of a world (like that considered by Oedipa Maas in Pynchon's *The Crying of Lot 49*), it moves from its modernist home base into the zone of postmodernism.[53]

This same axis inheres in the fiction of William Gass and in part explains his impatience with readers who, on the one hand, are not sophisticated or self-demanding enough to puzzle along in his verbal tunnels, and his desire to have, on the other hand, a docile reader succumb to the power of his language,[54] to yield to authorial imposition of another consciousness like that a piece of music creates, to accept the author's special way of understanding reality,[55] to experience an ontological shift. We shall see this line crossed many times in the fiction of Gass. This frequent crossing establishes an epistemological-ontological continuum. Such a continuum between seeming polarities makes of Gass a writer who occupies not a middle ground of synthesis, but a constantly shifting and indeterminant zone between outer limits. Gass seems to understand this continuum better than most of the more intransigent metafictionists like Katz and Sukenick; he therefore is reluctant to say that he has turned his back on one or the other side of the question. As a "purified modernist," he transcends his announced "radical"[56] stance, preferring instead to write, not merely revolutionary, but lasting fiction. This vibration between literary outlooks is one element of his combativeness; he thinks, speaks, and writes from many directions. He pits himself against many foes. His way of writing, as well as his basic nature, is confrontational.

Narrative Structure

Confrontation and conflict engender Gass's narrative structure. Like his characters (who grow out of a proper name [*FFL*, 37]), the narrative emerges from a verbal center, in most cases from a title. The title or a few key words establish the central metaphor.[57] All his stories except his first one, "The Pedersen Kid," which Gass says started with a story line, are developed from an idea—an image from daily life like a roach or an icicle or a rock skipping across the surface of water.[58] As soon as he exposes "a symbolic center," he has finished the work. That is where, he says, whatever unity there is in his fiction comes from. Spiralling or tunneling out from the center involves not writing, comments Gass, but rewriting. He starts with a sentence, writes it over again many times, and adds other sentences to expand the original idea. Eventually paragraphs and pages appear.[59] This time-intensive process of organic growth outward from the center, as opposed to linear development, not only requires that the author stew over his sentences and his paragraphs but demands as well that the reader loiter in the language, soak up the ambience of the story space as one would sit in a bus station and breathe in its diesel fumes, sweat, and tobacco smoke.

Moving along some invisible wire that skewers episodes of the narration that in turn generate plot is not Gass's way. In his debate with John Gardner, who insists that plot is necessary to story and that the author must create in the reader's mind a "vivid and continuous dream," Gass likens narrative structure to a house: the reader, who can stop midway or go back to the entrance, is pushed along by the author through a building of words.[60] Gardner admits that the reader will seldom be able to sit out a plot for several hours or days of uninterrupted concentration; people can rarely read two hundred pages without some kind of break. But literature for Gardner is like a piece of music on a phonograph record. Although the listener (reader) can stop the record at any point, leave, and then return to it, he still must be able to find a distinct and gently beckoning groove in which to reinsert the phonograph needle. The reader needs an immediately identifiable path through the work. The pathway that the plot affords the reader, what Gardner calls the "feeling of profluence, of forward flowingness," leads to an honest, gentle "exploration" of a given fictional situation, an "act of faith," a "love relationship with the reader."[61] Gardner makes an excellent point, a point that is an indictment of the bulk of radical metafictionist theory: "When you decide as a writer that the novel is just a house you're trying to get somebody to go through in various ways, you have broken faith with the reader because you are now a manipulator, as opposed to an empathizer. If the novelist follows his plot, which is the characters and the action, if he honestly and continuously proceeds from here to here because he wants to understand some particular question, the reader is going to go with him because he wants to know the same answers. On the other hand, if the writer makes the reader do things, then I think he puts the reader in a subservient position which I don't like."[62]

Although Gass responded that manipulation of readers was not what he meant by the house analogy, Gardner did, nevertheless, point out a worrisome strand: Gass does attempt to dominate readers. One instance of Gass's confession to an "indictment" of his audience is his comparison of forcing readers to accept a monster (and to admit the monstrousness in themselves) with what he calls the "bail-tail trick."[63] This classroom device works by taking a notion that students accept without thinking, and then by subjecting that belief to critical reasoning (that students have been taught to follow), the bias is either unseated or the reasons for accepting it are clarified. Gass wants readers (like students) of "The Tunnel" to accept Kohler's unacceptable notions[64] and then carry those suppositions through their logical consequences, seeing in the end the viciousness hidden beneath the surface of seemingly simple ideas. This is without doubt an offensive view of rhetorical (authorial) power; it was offensive to Athenians when Socrates engaged in it. Even Gass himself, although not apologetic of this novel's more sociopolitically direct purposes, expresses his reservations. He admits to manipulating his readers and expresses his ambivalence toward such tactics.[65] The point is that this kind of approach is a good teaching method, one indispensable in a philosophy classroom. And one of the dominant drifts of postmodernist fiction is didacticism. This teaching emphasis reflects a rebirth of allegory in contemporary writing.

Modern critics such as Edwin Honig, Angus Fletcher, Paul de Man, and Maureen Quilligan point to a resurgence of allegory in the latter years of this century.[66] Quilligan attributes the resurfacing of allegory in postmodern prose to the growing linguistic awareness and emphasis on word-play that I have discussed. The "sacralizing" power of words, as in the medieval period, has resulted in the verbal imposition of another world, a superrealism of metaphor taken seriously.[67] This ontological orientation fits McHale's definition of postmodernism; he carries his definition into new branchings, distinguishing the postmodern allegory as "transparent . . . offering apparently no obstruction to interpretation," and "Manichaean": "Variations on the venerable mode of psychomachia, these allegories typically involve the confrontation of warring principles, semantic oppositions personified. . . . Where ancient psychomachias characteristically pitted personified Good against personified Evil, however, the postmodernist versions tend to prefer the Nietzschean opposition between the Apollonian and Dionysian principles, rational order vs. mindless pleasures."[68] These "polar opposites," writes McHale, actually parodies of allegory or "mock allegories," are "allowed to 'bleed' into one another," their "symmetries" thus "systematically undone."[69] As we shall see, Gass creates precisely this kind of "mock" allegory, an extension of the metaphorical force of his characters into what passes for plot in his fiction. In the chapter on *Omensetter's Luck,* I will refer to this oppositional delineation of character and story as "syzygy," an astronomical term that describes the rectilinear alignment of heavenly bodies. Since Gass, like John Fowles, often makes use of Hermetic or occult terminology (especially in "The Tunnel" and *Omensetter's Luck*), I prefer to use the Hermetic (Chaldean or astrological) meaning of syzygy: the mutual sharing of traits between entities diametrically placed. This definition is similar to Yeats's gyre and the circular symbol of yin-yang. Gass's oppositional structuring of his writing matches the confrontational and dual persona of the "tame wild man."

Working "against the grain" is an understandable ethos. Taking liberties with established expectations about art as well as about politics, morality, education, the law, and the American way of life in general is the way of the revolutionary. Going counter to old ways and traditional notions about things leaves us sometimes with the impression that the one who sets himself against tradition considers himself possessed of greater knowledge and skill than the average person can boast. Along with Gardner, I sense this superiority and this aloofness in William Gass. But, as I have said, Socrates was similarly thought of and rightly so: this is the inevitable position of the professor before his students; teachers are by calling "opposers" who profess to know and who direct their disciples. And, of course, innovative writers (Cervantes is the prime example) have not ceased to deride and rework outworn forms as one step in the creation of new ones. That cultural evolution necessitates, as a first move, a challenge of the established state of affairs is a truism. There can be no real progress without iconoclasm; and the iconoclast must break an icon or two. What worries John Gardner and other more traditional writers and critics about William Gass and the surfictionists of the sixties radical novel are their pronouncements; in most cases, particularly in the case of Gass, their work softens their sometimes strident dicta. Metafictionists like Gass whose work has perdured into the 1980s have not in an absolute or fanatical way stuck to any theoretical egregiousness. Their fiction, like all valid writing, has moved along the multistranded lines of dialectic, the fundamental axes of literature: subjective and objective, epistemological and ontological, realist and antirealist, modernist and postmodernist, and so on.

A Sneaky Moralist

John Gardner saw behind the scenes of this verbal "showdown on Mainstreet" with his antagonist. He understood that there is at least a faint touch of the old-fashioned realist in Gass. Although Gass insists, at times harshly, that fiction should not reflect the real world, and therefore should not attempt any moral commentary on the daily life of human beings, his books, says Gardner, "end in magnificent affirmation" of humanity; that, in Gardner's view, is moral statement. Therefore, Gardner, along with other readers and critics,[70] occasionally finds himself at odds with the literary axioms of William Gass, dicta at times overly aggressive and direct in their attack on realist conventions, pronouncements that strike some as a bit arrogant and disdainful of average reader expectations. But although Gardner opposes Gass on theoretical grounds, and reproves him for "wasting the greatest genius ever given to America by fiddling around," he finds (as I do) "what he can do with language" to be "magnificent."[71]

Chapter Two
Omensetter's Luck:
"A Song Dancing in the Mind"

The title of William Gass's first—and to date only—published novel is at least partly deceptive in implying that the principal character of the book is named Omensetter; and its down-to-earth, colloquial beginning suggests that the word "luck" confirms its meaning to the everyday, popular level. It is not Brackett Omensetter at all, of course, but Jethro Furber, a wordmongering frontier minister, who is the leading voice (and therefore, for Gass, the hero) of the work.

The story of *Omensetter's Luck* can be summarized in a few sentences. An old man, Israbestis Tott, tries to remember and accurately relate the tale of Omensetter, a happy, confident, and carefree craftsman, who comes to settle with his wife and two daughters in Gilean, a late-nineteenth-century Ohio town. Like the two most powerful astrological setters of omens, the conjunction and the opposition, the town (following somewhat the lead of Henry Pimber, who tries to be exactly like Omensetter) at first is charmed by the newcomer; but then (under the power of Furber, the minister who viciously opposes Omensetter) turns against him, blaming him for the death (by suicide) of Pimber. This tension in Gilean disappears when the two antagonists, the settler and the preacher, both leave town; the resulting equilibrium is symbolized in the person of the new minister, a well-balanced, ordinary man. Just as the rather loose and farfetched plot of *Hamlet* serves as mere scaffolding for the rhetorical vigor of the prince's monologues, Gass's novel weaves its episodic convolutions into a central platform for the discourse of the Reverend Jethro Furber, the only fully developed character in the book. Surprisingly, in the twelve years that Gass labored over *Omensetter's Luck,* the loquacious cleric had no part in the text until the very last moment; not until the manuscript had been stolen, and then by necessity rewritten, did the reverend appear. Even so, Gass, in the second version, had intended at most only a small area of operation for Furber—that of a minor character; but the deliberate, moment-to-moment, sentence-by-sentence manner of composition that Gass practices opened a fissure in the novel's structural dike and the torrent of Furber's words gushed out, washing away or transforming practically all else. Furber turned out to be a natural and indispensable narrative force, an unstoppable outgrowth in the development of the novel's theme: the overwhelming problems attached to the desire to represent the world in words and the consequences of innocence in a fallen world. But a wordsmith without a counterpoised wordless one has no potential for development; words without referents can have no meaning; evil manifests itself only in its opposition to good.

As I have stated, the word *luck* in *Omensetter's Luck* transcends its common meaning; it spreads into catacombs of aesthetic and ontological significance. It is the middle ground between innocence and experience, animal and human, love and hate, selfless bliss and painful self-awareness, life and death, paradise and separation from God; it is the battleground between the forces of Omensetter and those of Furber. Luck is not, in this sense, a synthesis of opposites, but a vinculum, or as Gass has Furber put it, the elastic thread that breaks the fall of Satan from Heaven (74–75). Brackett Omensetter's luck is the core of the basic metaphor of art, indeed all that being alive on planet Earth implies. It is the road between being and not being.

Metaphor has many definitions and descriptions, but one fits the case of this novel perfectly: metaphor is the transforming of ordinary words into great systems of meaning. As David Jones would say, it is the transubstantiation of worn-out, worthless verbal junk into vibrant new signs, of the cursed things, the *Anathemata,* into sacred elements.[1] Gass performs the same kind of operation on any standard lexicon of vocabulary items—he seeks to infuse new life into old words and to resurrect buried shades of meaning and sound. He builds with these word-blocks levels of metaphor that can then wind around the central themes of the book, themes that are themselves embedded in greater metaphors and archetypes.

Character development, as a narrative device in *Omensetter's Luck,* is grounded in metaphor building. A character in literature, for Gass, is the noise of a name and the resultant rhythms and meanings that are suggested by and grow out of it. (*FFL,* 49). Furber, Omensetter, Pimber, Tott, and all the others are projection points of sounds, the sounds made by the reader if he reads out loud, the sounds that reverberate in his brain if he reads silently; they are places in the text where language may appear. They are also collection points for words; language in a novel "eddies" around a name or an event, as that of Melville loops back to Ahab and his link with the whale (*FFL,* 49). These characters function allegorically; as word centers they stand for basic parts of the controlling metaphor itself (the duel between Omensetter and Furber and the deeper meaning that surrounds it).

The Omensetter–Furber opposition draws in two minor characters, Pimber and Tott; the four form a *quaternio* of interaction that allows Gass to re-present and reiterate the archetype of being as a wheel or a circle, as William Blake does in his painting *Michael and Satan*. The eternal struggle of opposites (in the case of the Blake painting, the Archangel Michael pitted against Satan) is best presented as a circular arena of struggling contraries most abstractly formalized in the yin-yang mandala or the quadrants of the zodiacal wheel. John Fowles makes extensive use of this oppositional and circular development of characters in his *The Ebony Tower* and *The Magus*. Gass relies on this method to allow his characters to turn slowly in the reader's mind, attracting as the narrative progresses the various shards that will fall into the controlling vortex of imagery. The novel constantly turns back to an archetypal (innocence versus self-awareness) core as it moves forward.

To reinforce the allegorical development of the characters in *Omensetter's Luck,* Gass resorts to a ringing musicality. The long chain of the symbolist movement, a formalist orientation to literature that emphasizes verbal musicality (particularly in poetry, but certainly including prose fiction), is made up of a number of links, William Gass among them,[2] that stretch from the time of Edgar Allan Poe, the head link and founder, through the nineteenth century (Valéry, Mallarmé, Baudelaire, Rimbaud) to the modern era (Woolf, Yeats, Eliot, Pound, Stein) and even to the present-day poststructuralists and metafictionists. Gass, after the manner of Stein and in his quest to write fiction that can be apprehended as a "totality," finds in music the perfect analogy for composition in a nonlinear style. Although literature is perceived sequentially, words, like musical notes, can be arranged as clusters, "chordal registers," allowing for a center of constant references and recall. In other words, one scene (a composite of words and symbols) can recall another one "so that the two are packed together."[3] Terms like "chordal register" and "packing in together" of themes and nuances of symbolic statement are important ones in the analysis of Gass's style in *Omensetter's Luck* and elsewhere.

Sound provides another structural possibility for this novel: musicality punctuates Gass's efforts to parody a classical American narrative form, the folktale or yarn, and a conventional American theme, the "nature–culture" dichotomy of the western. Limerick, children's song, folk song, popular hymns, and the traditional lyrical language of tale-telling call attention constantly to the form of the folktale, infusing it with a gravity and an additional level of poetic cohesion.

The rhythm that comes from the chainlinking of words forces us to recall what is suggested by the words in a special way, a way that the writer can control. That is to say that, in Gass's words, "the fictional quality of our sentences has little relation to their logical form."[4] The form is largely a matter of sequential order; sentences, like knotted ropes pulled through hands, set in motion vibrations that determine the firing order of images in the listener's brain. Even lists have their beat and their jingle: lists, like all utterances, are word fields where lovers of language, "the vowel-swollen cheek, the lilting, dancing tongue" can "wallow."[5] According to Gass, the sounds of a sentence are "its bones . . . good old dum dum dum de dump" (*WWW*, 331).

"Dum Dum Dum De Dump"

Very few pages in *Omensetter's Luck* lack the pounding rhythm that sets the "dum diddy dum dum, dum daaaa"[6] or "tongue . . . wink tick chew tock, wink wink" (88) going in the reader's mind, rhythmically tying sentence to sentence and paragraph to paragraph throughout the book. Sometimes Gass, as in the above passages (taken from two consecutive pages), overtly marks out the beat. Often the rhythm is more complex. The following lines illustrate the variety of cadences in the novel, from the explicit to the more subtle:

You've waited too long, now what's her name's begun, de dum de dum de dum de dum: we rise to praise the living God. Oh no indeedy. Incorrect. The third stone, reddish, small, flat with rounded edges and a glacial nick—the first two having fallen grievously short—was thrown by a ferrety boy in a sailor suit. It skipped twice before turning toward its target, then twice more, quickly, striking the giant between the eyes so that he fell with a groan, shaking the earth. There was generous applause and considerable shouting. A pillar of dust rose from beneath the body, two thousand sneezing. With the clangor of arms the armies collided. Yar. Yar. Yar. (88)

The initial and the final lines of this passage seem to be rhythmic just for the fun of it. And that is the case with much of the novel; there is a delight to be found in mere vocalization. Nonsense syllables and words normally keep the beat but cannot be considered as vehicles for great meaning. The last sentence, followed by the three "Yars," at first reading has the appearance of gratuitous wordplay. It is composed of a pair of anapests, then an iamb after a caesura, and finally another anapest plus a final beat (dum dum DUM, dum dum DUM, dum DUM, dum dum, DUM dum), balanced with similar word pairings on each side: "clangor"–"arms," "armies"–"collided." It is

pleasing to say. But this phrase also connects with the middle of the passage
and helps round it out. The clangor of armies refers to the battles and killings
constantly described in the Bible, the only book his parents deem safe enough
for the fragile, unbalanced child named Jethro Furber. He fears the stones
that fly at the victim in the story of the "stoned man," and these stones suggest also the death of Goliath at the hand of a young king. The image of
David with his sling melds also with the boy in the sailor suit who throws the
rock that hits young Jethro as he runs from a group of children playing king-
of-the-mountain. These images, like stones, assault the adult Furber as he recalls his childhood experience at a tent meeting.

The beat of the sentences on these two pages of text unites these biblical
scenes in Furber's mind, terrifying young Jethro and making the grown-up
Reverend Furber stop to reflect on the stone that sails through the air and
kills, and the heads of the kings and of Absalom hanging in trees, and the
"ringlet of leaves" around Abner's head—all these things are associated with
other children with whom Furber played the rough, battlelike game of push-
ing and beating others off a hill. One of them chants a children's rhyme,
picking up the rhythm:

> hingledy
> dingle-dy
> his is so sing-a-ly
> if we go single-ly
> we'll find the crown
> (89)

As children suddenly begin throwing rocks, little Jethro is hit before he can
stumble into the arms of his parents, crying that he had seen "Absalom alive
in the oak" (89). His parents, realizing the uncontrollable power of their son's
imagination, vow to keep him away from excessive theological preoccupation, and especially evangelistic meetings. This series of lines, begun with
nonsense "meter" words, enhances the presentation of the principal character,
a weak, alienated, paranoid youngster whose imagination feeds on the images of death and destruction that he culls from his Bible readings: heads
hanging in trees and heads thrown from walls like stones.

The jingle moves the rhetoric from biblically infused images to an account
of what really happened to little Jethro (hit by a rock thrown by another
child), just as another children's song introduces this section ("Willie the
whiny, / his nose nice and shiny, / will die, die, die" [85]), and moves the
time frame from the adult Furber's ruminations about the headstone of Pike

in the garden of his church back to a similar "revelation" about death and stones and leaves and trees that he had had "once before" in childhood (86). The narrator explains the process straightforwardly: "Through his head, to the tunes of children's songs, his pitiful beliefs, his little sentences of wisdom, danced foolishly as he dozed, the meters they were forced to skip to reducing them to a vulgar gibberish. He tried to rally his thoughts and form them in unassailable squares, but not a line would hold, they broke ahead of any shooting and the Logos wandered disloyally off, alone" (85).

This scene typifies Gass's presentation of character by means of word and rhythm: the adult Jethro lets his mind climb back along the pathway of images, the tone, the tree, the leaves, and the established story structures of the Bible to reach a pivotal moment in his life as a character, a verbal center, a man immersed in theological "squares," impregnable to all but death and all the reminders, both past and present, of its dynamic haunting. The beat sets it all up and allows us to savor the whirling images and their interconnection with others as the narrative moves in many directions and folds itself into layers and "chords."

Another deft portrait driven by meter is that of Dr. Orcutt in the blacksmith shop, destroyer (in the name of science) of folk medicine. The beat is launched by a litany of old wives' tales about diseases and folk cures, beginning with what has become the talk of the town, Omensetter's "lucky" nature healing of Pimber and of his own finger: "Orcutt aimed his spit / Let's see that finger Matthew smashed / You're a bastard, Truxton, Watson said / You took on so, I thought I'd see / Well, Brackett? No charge for curiosity. The nail grow back? Mat told me that he knocked it clean away—is that a fact? / Omensetter held his hand out silently / Orcutt grinned . . . Orcutt dropped the hand" (48). The dum de dum of the lines again is music in itself, especially as it combines with the rhyme (joining "see," "curiosity," and "silently") and assonance (connecting "back" with "fact" and "smashed"); but again, there is method here, function in the fun. The seeing of the curious doctor and the silence of Omensetter bring about a major change in the direction of Omensetter's luck. Once the doctor has questioned the "home remedy" ("by god—it's killed an awful lot" [49]) and has labeled it as such, a part of the miraculous healing, the growing back of the nail, smashed by the clumsy hammer-slip of Watson that would be called unlucky for most but is the *felix culpa* that has driven out the steel sliver and the pus and thus has been transformed by the innocent naturalness of Omensetter into "luck," the spell is broken. The "fact" of the "smashing" is that, now, in the presence of the spitting Orcutt, who antipathetically spits at the notion of taking real luck (coincidence) for miracle, the unreal, magical luck of Omensetter manifests itself. Meter, image, rhyme, and assonance work together to make up this pivotal portrait and scene: it underscores the ironic fact that in the end, plain, down-to-earth Dr. Orcutt (once Omensetter becomes aware of the limitations of his own unconscious powers) will turn out to be the only hope for saving the life of Omensetter's son.

Another poetic device that Gass calls into service to bolster his character development is alliteration. Furber, at the moment of seducing Watson into believing that Omensetter's luck is really the work of the devil, recites a list of jingling words, lost cities of the ancient world. He then comments on the futility of human life and the inevitable oblivion that awaits all people, linking the principal symbols with alliteration:

All those cities, those hollow houses, all those lives, those graves the graves of hope . . . With a madness like the madness to bury that seizes men, a craze to cover that overcomes all of them, the cities covered themselves with sand and mud, vines, grass, lava, with noisier cities, completer ruins, further graves and further grasses. I am their proper lordship, Furber thought. My credentials make me master of the resting places. That was the way—burial to burial, shame to shame—it had always been since Adam's fig had hidden him, his sex and death together and the same, and surely that was the way it would continue. He—Furber—would be lost in a swallow of persons. The stone in the corner of his garden would not truly speak of him, the great Leviathan would have him, he'd be buried in their bodies—cover after cover coming—for that was the whole of life on the earth, our bodies for a time athwart another's middle, our lives like leaves, generation after generation lifting the level of the land, the aim of each new layer the efficient smother of the last. (139)

These lines reiterate the stone/leaf motif, and alliteration braids together its parts. For instance, "life on the earth" is made up of "our lives" that "like leaves" lift the "level of the land" as each new "layer" buries the "last." This "smothering" relates to the alluvial burying of ancient cities, great centers of human activity and spirit, that yield to the deadly cycle of time ("cover after cover coming") in the same way human beings succumb to the stoniness of death, and deposit their bodies in the ground like falling leaves that once hung alive in trees like the sons of kings, like Absalom (and like Henry Pimber). Furber sees himself as a master of the garden, the warden of the "craze to cover" that seems to find embodiment in the stone and Leviathan, biblical markers of individual as well as world apocalypse. Adam's leaf, a covering that "had hidden him," that had hidden his sex, and therefore had hidden his mortality (for procreation ultimately is but the forerunner of death, the generation of one's replacement), is injected neatly into the main body of the novel's leaf symbolism. Thus, in alliterative chains of words, the scheme of *Omensetter's Luck,* the reworking of the sad archetype of Eden, is reintroduced.

Form and Folktale: A Structure for Parody

The metafictional impulse is to do again one last time things that have been overly done so that there can be an end to them as conventions and clichés and so that new life can be breathed into them. Parody is the natural method of all innovative novelists in one sense: most writers desire to forge ahead with something new—something that goes against the old and the worn-out. Gass's challenging of convention thus underlies the genesis of the structure of *Omensetter's Luck*: he superimposes his new story upon that of a worn-out mode, that of the tall tale or the folk story. Chapter 1 begins with a string of sentences that directly reflect this tradition, even if in a more poetic fashion than is usually found in vernacular literature: "Brackett Omensetter was a wide and happy man. He could whistle like the cardinal whistles in the deep snow, or whir like the shy 'white rising from its cover, or be the lark a-chuckle at the sky. He knew the earth. He put his hands in water. He smelled the clean fir smell" (31).

American legend provides the perfect structural vehicle for Gass's parody of the civilization/barbarity cliché. The idea of legend, like myth, is rooted in Eden and the Fall of Man. Duncan Enrich, however, explains why, in American folklore, there are no genuine myths: "Myths (in the folk and literary sense) deal with stories about the Creation, of how man came into being, how fire was brought to earth, and such. When the first ships from Spain and England touched shore in Florida, Virginia, and Massachusetts, they brought with them passengers who had passed well beyond any Greek need for such beautiful believings."[7] According to Robert A. Georges, legend, unlike myth, takes place in time, in history. Myth has no time because it is not tied to the physical generation of actual men, to the genealogical pattern begun in the Garden. Once there are people who beget people, there is history, not myth. The colonists had come to populate; their arrival was a matter of record. Georges writes that what we mean by "history," however, is relative: "The time during which Eve lived is considered to be in the *recent past* by some, in the *remote past* by others, and *never* by still others; and the historical or antihistorical character of the past depends upon whether or not one regards Eve and/or God as 'historical personages.'"[8] Gass takes Georges's "open-ended" view of legend in the writing of *Omensetter's Luck*: that history is ambiguous; that, to quote Georges again, the *past* of a legend may be "*either* recent *or* remote and *either* historical *or* antihistorical; and while a legend is set in the *past,* it might really be conceived to be *in* and *of* the *present.*"⁹ This folkloric insecurity about the nature of history and legend (fiction, narrative, storytelling) is personified in the character Israbestis Tott whose ramblings and attempts to piece together the events and impressions surrounding the phenomenon of Omensetter aptly begin the novel, a parody, or a reworking of the legend.

A subtype of American legend has been classified as the "saint's tale," a term from medieval lives of the saints, created and preserved largely through oral tradition. These stories were transplanted to American soil by many groups, particularly by those from Central Europe and Germany. Don Yoder has studied one class of saint's tale popular among the Swiss and German groups of Pennsylvania: the many variations spawned by the story of *die hei-lige Genoveva* (Saint Genevieve of Brabant).¹⁰ Saint Genoveva, who had been a cult figure in the lower Rhineland, is said to have been an innocent nobleman's wife accused of infidelity by an evil jester or court poet because he, the slanderer, could not seduce her. Her husband believed the lies. Carrying her young son, Genoveva was driven away into the deep trees of the forest where she managed to survive and live at peace among the animals. She at last was vindicated and allowed to return home where she lived happily for the rest of her life. The evil jester (or poet) was drawn and quartered.

In addition to the standard struggle between an innocent nature queen who is nourished by the forest and the animals (she appears in some paintings standing nude before a cave) and a civilized court liar whose vicious fabrications are taken to be true, there is the underlying implication of health derived from purity. Yoder links the Pennsylvania "brand of occult folk-medicine, which uses charms in the attempt to heal the ills of man and beast," with these saints' tales.¹¹ We see immediately in this tale the skeleton of the legend of Omensetter. Innocent and trusting, maligned by Furber the word-twisting deceiver, Brackett unsuspectingly enters into a contest of personality with the reverend by virtue, in large part, of the former's kinship with the animal life force, his occult healing powers, and his supposed clairvoyance (his setting of omens).

This category of storytelling is the *materia* from which the romanticized "Old West" or frontier yarn grew. As the frontier epoch drew to a close, folk literature branched out in many directions; one of these led to the stock western, featuring the hackneyed plot structure built on a duel between the bad men and the good men, between the black-hatted villain and the white-hatted hero. By the sixties, with the opportunity afforded by television and film for most people in the United States to have mentally ingested and re-gurgitated a substantial stock of such pulp, this stereotype had descended into trite, insipid convention. It is this worn-out form that Gass seeks to poke fun at (and at the same time to resuscitate, by means of parody and brilliant, musical language).

Like the tinny melodies of a player piano pinging away on the soundtrack of a western movie, Gass's collection of vernacular poetry and folk rhymes,[12] saturated with the feverish, sex-intoxicated idiosyncrasy of Furber's rehash of them, reverberates in the background of the novel.

Cheek resting on the pages of his open Bible, agonizing like an embarrassed child about his poor conduct of the church service just concluded, Furber signals his pianist, Mrs. Spink, to begin playing a hymn and listens to the "rattle of notes" as she begins. As he tries to find the number of the hymn, "the number of the noise . . . so numerous . . . numberless numbering . . . numb . . . numb . . . what was the numb. . . ?" (171), he recites to himself one of the many childish ditties in the novel, rope-skipping jingles that folklorists call counting rhymes: "Spink'll soon tinkle her tune to a stop / end in a jiffy her jiggery hop" (171), which calls to mind a New England form in the Botkin anthology—"Onery, uery, ickory, a, / Hallibone, crackabone, ninery-lay."[13] In this scene, the protected, innocent, and now-vanished childhood of the inwardly turned Furber is a momentary refuge from "the richness of his robes and the weight of his responsibilities" (171). Again, the contrast between childish silliness and adult gravity is reinforced in the rhythm and rhyme of Gass's prose.

The folkloric cohesion of the novel is aided by the lacing in of what Gass himself calls "fragments of dancehall song" (130), music that recalls the general historical period of *Omensetter's Luck*: "Imagine my distress / if you undo my dress / for if you do, / oh me! undo / for if you do, / oh my! untie— / then I'm undone, / I must confess; I'll simply die / without my dress" (130). Echoing the acoustic difference and interrelation of chords and notes, or drone and melody (as with banjos and bagpipes), the seduction theme of the song provides a background rhythm for the narration and dialogue of Furber's verbal seduction of Mat Watson (into believing that Omensetter's luck is evil). This kind of interplay recalls the double-entendre dialogues of *Madame Bovary* staged against other kinds of discourse—for example, Rodolphe's erotically tinged verbiage spoken as he and Emma listen to patriotic bombast at the fair. Another modified children's rhyme that throbs in the background and is at the same time functional in the internal development of the novel is the variation of "Ding Dong Bell, Pussy's in the Well":

Ding dong bell,
   Pimber's down our well.
   Henry tried to urge his horse into a run, but on the badly rutted road, in the poor light, it refused. He cursed a moment, and gave up. Who pushed him in?
   Little Henry Pim.
   Omensetter was no better than an animal himself. That was right. And Henry wondered what it was he loved, since he thought he knew what he hated.
   Who'll pull him out?
   Nobody's about.
   What Omensetter did he did so simply that it seemed a miracle. It eased from him, his life died, like the smooth broad crayon line of the man who drew your cartoon at the fair. He had an ease impossible to imitate, for the moment you were aware, the instant you tried. (42)

The background rhythm set by the familiar verses grounds the narrative, Pimber's anguished interior monologue, in the universal self-oblivion of childhood, and linguistically encapsulates, as does almost every page of the book, the central theme of life's perplexing duality. Any reader who has grown up speaking English in America has inherited these nursery rhymes, and therefore is the receiver of set forms, integrals of meaning and association, that bind common experience with the deeper layers of childhood. Gass's appropriation of a linguistic given, a set pattern (analogous to the philosophical notion of a priori), is perfectly consistent with his way of working outward from a conceptual nucleus; it is also an ingenious way of uniting the theme with familiar music. In other words, a recast children's verse incorporates the singsong simplicity of mindless ease of being with the carnal knowledge that carries with it an awareness of the purpose of sex, that is to say, an ultimate death. Pimber, trying to achieve the animal grace and carelessness of Omensetter, realizes that "the instant you were aware, the instant you tried," is the instant in which the self is doomed—there can be no return to Eden. Unlike animals, humans live in time, ticking off to themselves a finite number of days of life until the end. Unlike humans, the fox in the well, although in folklore presented as the craftiest of animals, "had never measured off his days in moments; another-another-another" (42).

   The wall around Eden, then, is time, and the only path of evolution is from animal to human, not the reverse. Pimber cannot be a fox and he cannot be Omensetter. Pimber can only retrace in his mind the journey from oblivion to hyperawareness of time, from animal to human, from Omensetter to Pimber: having fallen farther into himself, he can, in his imagination, "pass from animal to Henry, become human in his prison, X his days, count, wait, listen for another" (42). In these lines, Henry Pimber is contrasted sharply with the automatic, uncritical (yet survivalist) self-immersion of the animal world: he lacks the apparent wisdom of a horse that refuses to run over bad terrain at night; he lacks the natural miracle-working ability of Omensetter who heals with ease and unconcern.

Thus, an innocent little folk song, a ditty about children's cruelty to animals (the drowning of a cat in a well) that all of us recognize, is made to summarize the deepest of all ontological questions, that of being and time. Gass has used the duality inherent in the rhyme, the cruelty that exists side by side with what adults romanticize as blissful childishness, to reiterate his theme and at the same time to continue the beat of the language.

The Voice from the Stone

The rhythm of folk literature helps establish a character (absentee foil for Furber) named Andy Pike. The Reverend Andrew Pike, the ghost that dominates the brain of Jethro Furber, was the pioneer minister of the Gilean, Ohio, church where Furber has been assigned. His life is Furber's imaginary creation brought forth from a vine-covered stone, a burial marker that stands out cleanly from the other gravestones in the church garden because of Jethro's careful weeding and because of its words, ordinary, simple, but which "sound well" (96) and are the kernel of a made-up spirit that both inspires and mocks Furber's ministry in Gilean. Having "scrubbed the faces" of the markers, Furber redeems Pike's epitaph from the oblivion of weeds and vines, able finally to read and meditate upon the provocative fragment:

> Rev A dy Pike
> when his churc
> was a cabin
> die o his love
> 18 9
>   (83)

Unlike the other inscriptions ("stupid and dull, lines of sweet memorial cant"), the Pike fragment, into which Furber is obliged by his fictive mentality to pour much more than just the few letters necessary to complete the basic meaning of the words, is the seed of a dominant metaphor: Pike as a fish. Furber, often "redeciphering" and "pondering" Pike's tombstone, ranges far beyond the local legends that the marker calls to mind: "vague, confused tales, anguished and full of disaster, passionate as the legend of this monument," creating a sound system that talks to Furber and seems to have a life of its own, even though the dead divine is merely a bundle of "bones in butcher's paper" (84), nothing but a literary character, a place from which language emanates.

The poetic speech of tombstones calls to mind the genre of folklore known as tombstone lyrics. Enrich has collected a number of these writings and has found that they fall into a variety of categories: "They range from admonition and warning to rough and macabre humor. Some are pathetic; others move to tears; some are thumb-nosingly caustic; all are informative."[14] And all contain a germ of life. The belief that the soul persists in stones, and therefore that the personality of the dead is somehow a part of a particular stone, surfaces from the depths of our collective primitive ancestry. M. L. von Franz writes that oval stones were associated with one's "innermost being, his true personality" and that Australian aborigines still believe that their ancestors continue to exist in stones.[15] Jung considers the stone to be symbolic of "individuation," of the transformed man, and of "the content of consciousness."[16] The idea of stone as symbolic of the numinous, transcendent self, a lasting permanence in the face of death's obliteration, appears extensively in *Omensetter's Luck;* it is the principal image in the novel.

Pike's epitaph provokes torrents of words and jingles (often nonsense) from Furber; these words unleash, in their ringing, the full "bunch" of associated elements of the Pike metaphor, the clusters of musical notes in the recurrent "chord" that is the "voice of an indian," the pristine source of frontier theology. Old Pike, unlike the socially awkward Furber, handles himself well with the ladies of the church: "Thanky kindly, Missus Spink, but if I do, I'll surely sink," (84). This sinking from Mrs. Spink's nut-laden brownies plays about the fish metaphor set to work by the name Pike (a common and voracious fish), who has died because he loved, because he "struck" the hook of life, lured by "grub or worm most likely, hardly fly" (84). The light trochaic beat of both lines amalgamates images of primitive Christianity: Christ as Fish, his disciples as the fishers of men, the baptismal loss of the old nature by ritual death (sinking) in the river, the real death in the river that Furber wishes for Omensetter (a counterpart of Pike—"Backett, you ought to like him. Howls when he feels the need" [84]), the sinker that sinks the hook and thereby brings about the death of the fish.

The Fish

Gass's choice of the fish as a dominant and recurring symbol is an interesting one. As C. J. Jung has shown, the historical and cultural, as well as the psychological, ramifications of the fish image are legion.[17] Time and place are the raw materials from which the fish symbol arises. In archaic religions, the north was a region of dread and evil. Jung, attempting to explain the paradox of the equal intensity of fear and veneration attached to the north (specifically why Sabaeans, Mandaeans, and ancient peoples of many lands turned northward to pray), says that "ancient history gives us a divided picture of the region of the north: it is the seat of the highest gods and also of the adversary; thither men direct their prayers, and from thence blows an evil pneuma . . . and finally, it is the navel of the world and at the same time hell."[18] This locus, this actual geographical region, is both hated and loved because it is the seat of time. Ancient time measurement was astrological, based on the zodiac of twelve divisions of the ecliptic. As the Earth moves in its orbit, it wobbles in a way that makes the poles trace a circle through the constellations. This imaginary circle is divided, like the zodiac, into twelve ages, the last of which is Pisces, the Age of the Fish. Jung says that according to the Apocalypse of Baruch, the time before the coming of the Messiah and the end of the world is divided into these twelve parts, and the Messiah appears in the twelfth. At this point, Leviathan rises out of the sea and battles Behemoth, a land monster; both beasts are components of Being or Yahweh. The monsters mortally wound each other; Yahweh cuts up their bodies and feeds the flesh to the faithful. This, says Jung, is a possible genesis of the old Jewish Passover (celebrated in the month of the fish, Adar) and in part gives rise to the fish as eucharistic food in early Christianity.[19]

Old Pike, the Fish, invites similar associations: he is a numen who comes to Furber from time, the past, a wilder, less civilized era (idealized in a kind of mountain-man legend); his memory is rooted in the graveyard in the church courtyard—he is the ideal priest of western expansion, a self-reliant half-savage, for Furber a type of paragon who speaks to Furber's imagination in messianic tones—he speaks of nature and love. He is not, like Furber, a prisoner of ecclesiastic verbiage. Gass, having confessed that he has no patience or skill with conventional plotting,[20] relies upon the continual play about this nuclear concept and its subdivisions for an important component of the thematic structure of *Omensetter's Luck*.

There is, naturally, a coarser extension of Pike as the Fish. He is the original "father" of the Gilean faithful, both in the sense of priest and patriarch, who, in his rough-and-makeshift simplicity harbors strong sexual motives to which he partially surrenders in a comic way, biting as vigorously at the cookies of Missus Hatstat as Adam "struck" at the fruit. Pike strikes, not at flies, carefully crafted wisps of unreal frilliness, but at fat worms, slimy crawlers of the loathsome kind that come to mind as we wonder "what it was he'd struck—grub or worm most likely, hardly fly" (84). Again the driving drum of the trochee ties this extension to the other fish images and then again to the stone. The cause of his death, "love" according to the gravestone, links with the sexual reference to Missus Hatstat's cookies: "Poor Pike must have bitten hard. The stone seemed to say so." These lines unite the established beat (DAHdah, DAHdah, dahdahDAH) with the sibilant harmony of the alliterated "s."

One of the "notes" of this metaphorical "chord," the image of the fish and the grub on the hook, recalls another text earlier in the book that both complements and replicates it:

Wasn't that the shadow of the hat, the hooks hanging? Or was it a moon in a green sky? There's the line come down, a homemade spinner, Knox's surely, a little rusty, the sinker's already clouding an inch of the bottom. What's he using, grubs? Fly maggots, maybe. Nothing heaves with life like they do. Two or three are forked on the hook like peas. Is it the channel cat he's after? Is that where I'm lying? Um. His spinner's dancing. Catches the eye. Revolving white haunches. What if I bit? (76)

This passage presents the same register of images that is found in the fish metaphor. And it offers reinforcement, by repetition, of the central trope. Omensetter's hat, a hat that has fishhooks stuck in it, has blown off the owner's head and landed in the water; people watch as the hat drifts on down the river. Furber imagines himself a fish looking up at the hat flowing by above. From the fish's-eye view, the hat is a moon in a green sky. It is full of collected light and, like the moon, it is the setter of omens and cycles of time and tides that mankind has always sought to read and interpret (and which, in the fleshly form of Omensetter, Furber must himself read and interpret). The lunar rotundity of the hat, like the globular fatness of the grub, carries with it a dangerous array of barbs that can destroy the fish. Furber, as another fish, as a disciple of Jesus the Fish and a successor of Old Pike, expresses his almost irresistible compulsion to bite at the white, fat worm, to yield to the desire to be a fish like Pike. Pike and Omensetter, both characters of action and forthright spirit, coalesce in the fish/bait/hook "chord"; to strike at the moon and to strike at the grub thus place Furber in an order of signs both repulsive and attractive to a preacher locked inside himself. Furber would indeed relish being a Pike in order to gulp at the fat white maggot on the hook, even if the hook resonated with mortal danger. Locked in his sterile world of words, Furber (like Pimber) could be rescued by becoming Pike, by surrendering to his natural self, by exposing himself to danger in striking at the bait of life. This many-leveled, sound-concatenated image of the Reverend Pike, a cluster rather than a stratification, hovers powerfully at this point in the novel.

In Furber's metaphorical recasting of Omensetter as the incarnation of evil, he extends his envy and hatred of the "broad and happy man" to Lucy Omensetter, with a violent jealousy now expressed as lust. As in Furber's release of Pike's ghost from the tomb through the dual image of the weed and the headstone, the reverie of sex with Omensetter's wife is given form in the union of leaves and stone. This time it is the stone of the wall that surrounds the garden, Furber's observation post, fused with the stone upon which Lucy sits, and the leaves of the ivy that covers the wall, the barrier that separates Furber (like his barrier of verbal foliation) from the burning sand near the river (to parallel the burning fertility of Lucy on a rock in the river). The long paragraph that begins with "Raucus ivy" and ends with "Joy to be a stone" (67) includes both the liturgical sentences of Furber's church service, held inside, and his vivid mental tableau in which Lucy, outside, with her dark nipples, swollen body, and white skin, sits sprawled on the rock with the other Omensetters, dangling her feet in the water.

Lucy's swollen, white body again suggests the white fat grub on the hook that Pike struck at, which is swollen like the full moon that sets the menstrual cycle that brings about the human life cycle, which is like Omensetter's hat that moves in the fish's eye as a barbed moon, and which Furber dreams of "striking" ("something to tipple from her mountainous nipple") as do both Omensetter (in Furber's mind) and Omensetter's son (68). The clinging together of stone and ivy, representing the interplay of sterility and fecundity, alienation and engagement, words and action, begins and ends this circular chord. Its tentacles reach out into the book, both forward and backward, providing a repeated interplay between life and lifelessness. It is interesting to note that the novel opens with grass, weeds, and trees, and ends with stones that "hit" but do not "hurt the feelings" (9, 37).

The Stone

Like the fish, the stone carries with it symbolic associations that come already established archetypally. This universality of the stone image makes it perfect as part of the metaphorical core of *Omensetter's Luck*. Gass, like Jung, makes extensive use of the stone as emblematic of the self. Again, as in the case of the fish symbolism, no evidence supports a direct Jungian influence in Gass's writing. Apparently, both writers run separate taps for material into this deep anthropological spring.

I have mentioned the epitaph on Pike's headstone as the nucleus of a "voice" that takes on the dimensions of a character within Jethro Furber's verbal stream. The four strongest characters, Tott, Pimber, Furber, and

Omensetter, are individualized and drawn together by means of the stone symbol. The character of Tott starts its development outward from the sound of his name (101), a name that calls to mind his "tottering" around in his house as though it were the structural equivalent of his past and doing his "best" ("bestis") to arrange the fuzzy images in his senile brain so that an accurate history may be told of the people of Gilean (19).

Like Benjy in Faulkner's *The Sound and the Fury,* Tott introduces the characters of the novel in a scatterbrained, incoherent manner, emphasizing the near impossibility of telling a "true" story, of imposing a veridical chronicity on the past. He, like Gass, diddles away in the corners of his house, weaving webs of narrative about both "actual" people of his hometown and fantastic creatures of his imagination. Tott tries mightily to get the past "right," to put it in story form; but his mind is uneven, sometimes overpowering, and sometimes not strong enough to hold it all: "Tale after tale he told, each many times over, getting them right or trying to, amazed at what he forgot and what he remembered" (18). His imagination draws him away from "reality" (at bottom nothing itself but an intensely personal fiction) into the pure fiction of his wallpaper. Like a spider on the wall, Tott totters along the two-dimensional designs of the paper as if the flat surface were a world: "A grease spot was a marsh, a mountain or a treasure" (16–17). But his gnawing realization that the substitution of this fictional existence cannot take the place of real life brings him awareness of the artificiality of his story world and with that awareness of the pain of disillusionment. Tott's inability to stay in the wall-world, as well as his inadequacy and lack of strength to take on a vigorous and healthy relationship with the day-to-day life around him, brings pain: "The pain struck without obstruction then, and he closed like a spider on it" (18).

The spider metaphor for Tott's character development and for the representation of the dangers of slipping into verbally induced solipsism is a splendid one. As Gass warns repeatedly, literature cannot be made to equal human experience; therefore, any empirical relationship between fiction and fact is impossible. Echoing Wittgenstein, Gass states metaphorically here, as in many other parts of his work, that the substitution of fiction for life leads to unhealthy withdrawal and eventually to the creation of an "interior language" that cannot be shared communally and therefore cannot be "affirmed" by surrounding human life—to repeat Gardner's admonition. Tott stands for the excess of fiction that possesses the power to lose itself in itself but does not have the intellectual rigor and the self-awareness to be at the same time its own redemption. Tott is a spider who weaves sticky webs that capture the floating motes of existence—names, faces, things, places—but once these elements of the story or the picture are caught, he has difficulty sorting them out and arranging them into a coherent whole. Like a web, his fictions screen out the world, leaving him in his corner to "diddle," to spin even more elaborate webbing to occult himself.

Because Tott, like Pimber, desires regeneration, and because regeneration means the destruction of the old self, he seeks, through the ritual of killing spiders on walls (himself), the dissolution of his spidery inner self. And this self, like the other three major "selves" in the novel, is symbolized by a stone. The spider that he is in the process of killing as he winds through the long monologue of the Tott chapter is called finally "longlegs, like a smooth pebble walking" (19). As Tott squashes the longlegs with his thumb, a little girl watches. As innocently full of life and confidence as Tott is self-consciously full of death and disorientation, the child applauds the smashing of such an unattractive creature, human or arachnid: "Good. I hate spiders. They crawl you up . . . They're nasty" (30).

There is also a stone and a nastiness in the middle of the metaphorical shaping of Henry Pimber. Like Furber, Henry meditates on the relationship between the stone of walls, the gravestone, and the spirit: "I shall be my own stone, then my dear, my own dumb memorial, just as all along I've been my death and burial, my own dry well—hole, wall, and darkness" (60). He thinks these things while he compares himself to Omensetter, his newly found model for his changed self. Comparison with the "happy man" only intensifies his rocky lifelessness, however. "I've scarcely been alive," he thinks to himself, and, following the thread of tombstone verse, he starts to compose his own epitaph: "Henry Winslow Pimber. Now dead of weak will and dishonest weather. Some such disease. How would that look carved on my stone?" (60).

This scene is juxtaposed by means of the stone image with the night in which Pimber killed the fox, and, by ritual and symbolic substitution, his old self. Killing the fox had given Henry Pimber "the same fierce heedless kind of joy" (43) that he had felt as a child on the occasion of his punching his father in the stomach for no apparent reason. This childish, gratuitous, insensitive (Omensetterish) slash at parental authority had been relived in the act of killing the fox—an animal that had fallen into a hole that he, Pimber, in his inattention to his responsibility as landlord, had left uncovered. Both Omensetter and Pimber, each in his own way, had willed the death of the fox: Omensetter, animallike, had intended for nature to take its course; Pimber, humanlike, let a killing instrument do the work. Allowing to die and shooting both lead to death; the two ways of willing death unite, even if only ritually, Omensetter and his disciple: "The man

[Omensetter] was more than a model. He was a dream you might enter"
(43). At the same time, by depriving Omensetter of his will (letting the fox
die naturally), Pimber had struck a blow at the lucky man just as he had
earlier hit his father: "He knew, of course, it was Omensetter he had struck
at" (43). To cement this intense love-hate relationship with Omensetter,
symbolic of man's love-hate relationship with the animal world (innocence,
Eden, childhood), Pimber picks up five stones, and, as he has observed
Omensetter do constantly, chucks them at the river.

The throwing of stones is a ritual repeated throughout the novel.
Omensetter seems to give life and weightlessness to the dead weight of rocks
as he makes them skip across the water: "Omensetter's stones dipped and
flew and lit like gulls upon the water" (65). Omensetter hurls stones into the
river during the church hour on Sunday morning; Furber, inside his church,
casts the words of his sermon into the ears of his parishioners. The two kinds
of throwing seem mutually exclusive. But Omensetter is soon tempted into
the church, invited by Furber to attend like all the other people, and he accepts the invitation. Omensetter, now on Furber's turf, is a target for the latter's words, to be launched like stones at the Goliath in the pew: "Behold, oh
Lord, your champion here, your fond believer . . . Yet when he came before
the congregation and took his place and book above it, preparing his words
for bearing on the subject, shaping his lips for strong sounds, his certainty
drew a hesitation, his strength a meekness, and his sounds came down as
softly as the gray birds building in the steeple" (115). The avian quality of
both stone and word, Omensetter's gull-like stones skipping over the river's
surface and Furber's gray-bird words bouncing over the sea of faces in the
congregation, unites the two men even in their difference and their conflict.
In each case the harsh force of the words and the stones is softened by the
"light touch" of skill and the airiness of vitality. "It was truly astonishing the
way his stones would leap free of the water and disappear into the glare . . .
He took their weight in his palm and recorded their edges with his fingers,
juggling a number as he walked and tossing the failures down before he
curled his index finger around their rims and released them as birds . . . And
it did seem a stone until it skipped from the water . . . effortlessly lifting . . .
then skipped again, and skipped, and skipped . . . a marvel of transcending
. . . disappearing like the brief rise of the fish, a spirit even, bent on escape.
Furber chose his own stones carefully too" (117). This is the climax of the
story, brought about by stone-as-spirit-and-word symbolism.

Omensetter's character reaches its maximum intensity as it is pitched
against that of the others; for Omensetter is merely one extreme point on the
spectrum of being. Pimber, for instance, in his imitation of Omensetter's

stone throwing, enters the ritual of the reanimation of the lifeless, securing thereby his return to the dominion of the living: Omensetter cures him with a simple poultice. But even though the "Noisy One" (Omensetter) could send stones and even horseshoes "aloft and the heart (rising) with them," his projectiles, stone or iron, always had to come down again. Pimber, lifted up by the power of Omensetter, "skips" over the "water" for a while, but eventually falls under, and this despite his supreme ritualistic action to become the opposite of a stone, a leaf, going aloft and staying there, unlike the stones and the horseshoes, swinging literally like Absalom from the limb. Absalom could not be David; Pimber could not be Omensetter. Omensetter's ritual rock throwing, nevertheless, provides a natural, primitive, pagan counterweight to Furber's word throwing inside the church.

Reentering the domain of the fish symbol as a sign of erosive and eventually apocalyptic time, Furber re-Furbishes the "garden," actually a kind of stone lake in which Pike's grave, his "stone ship," sails around him without going anywhere. Furber carries sixty large stones and sets them in a circle, like sixty minute-marks on a stone clock, and walks around them, ritually enacting the desire to animate the dead weight of each passing minute that leads to the end of life: "Now he strode briskly from stone to stone, circling the sixty. How differently we give the semblance of life to the stone" (117), he says, as he watches Omensetter cast stones at the river and remembers Pike as "nothing but a shadow himself, merely a thin dim swimming something alongside the boat, a momentary tangle, a thistle of light" (117). Furber, himself a victim of rock throwing at many levels, finally takes the place of David, servant of God, and throws sinkers (stones or lead pellets) at Omensetter's fishhook-encrusted hat, sinking it to the bottom the way he had imagined Pike sinking from the weight of the nuts in the cookies, symbols of his love.

But once Furber starts throwing missiles, he is ineluctably drawn by ritual power into performing another act: leaving his stone garden and entering Omensetter's ground. The narrative falls again into the language of legend: "One Sunday, before the service and against his custom, where the people gathered, he went out to Omensetter, Omensetter's dog, his wife and daughters, and he said, the crowd around him listening on, why don't you come to church, you come to town, why not attend the services instead of throwing stones at the water? And Omensetter smiled and said, why if you like, we will; so presently they did" (114).

Omensetter now enters Furber's territory; the two draw nearer one another along their common axis of opposition. After church, Furber and Omensetter shake hands, and the minister's small fingers are lost in the hugeness of Omensetter's. Furber, like Claggart on the deck with Billy

Budd, is aware of the charm of pure animal innocence (lack of self-consciousness) and catches himself in the act of falling under its spell. Having realized that he had "unwittingly mimicked Omensetter's habitual manner" (116), Furber recoils from his momentary appreciation of the warmth and unreflective magnetism of his opponent (who, as it turns out, does not even view himself as an opponent): "If this was a consequence of simply shaking hands, it made him a kind of deadly infection. I am inhabited, Furber said. Ah god, I am possessed" (116). Furber brands Omensetter's Edenic gracefulness and lack of malice as threatening, as "magic," instead of "luck," thereby perverting linguistically the ontological simplicity, the raw being of the "beast" who gazes steadily into the cleric's face as Furber shouts "Leave me, Omensetter, leave us all" (116). The people are guided by the parson's words and now label Omensetter, who resumes his stone skipping instead of going to church, "a godless man," and Furber preaches "against frivolity with heat" (117).

Furber, although having been effective in his verbal proscription of his enemy, cannot cleanse himself of the Omensetter contagion. He has transcended the limits, gone beyond the fence as he had done as a child (going near the fence that contained the vicious dog, going so near that he had fainted in fright). Omensetter, for Furber, is the dialectical "other" that he has created in his mind, a fictional character whom he calls "Backett," not Brackett Omensetter; Furber's fictionalized Backett is both evil and attractive—and above all, dangerous. Omensetter stands for the dream of returning to bliss, to the possibility of overcoming death: "Be above yourself, that's what we've urged—Pike, you and I—we hanker for the other side. We've no reason to complain, then, if our crotch is cracked by a hurdle. But I wonder—you might know now—is it a lie? What ease instead to melt into the body's arms and be one's own sweet concubine. And Omensetter? Is he, in his fashion, like us? Is it cruel to tease stones so?" (118). The ritual teasing of stones unites Furber (and his spiritual mentor Pike) with Omensetter.

Omensetter has unwittingly begun to "hanker for the other side," to long for something better, something unattainable really, because he has married Lucy and has had children. The moment he impregnates his wife, the moment he thereby starts the process of wrenching life from lifeless matter, is the moment that he begins his devolution from the bliss of pure *ontos,* pure "luck," as he and the people of Gilean call it. Omensetter, in order to provide a better opportunity for his children, particularly for his new son, must move to Gilean, leaving behind his "last and happy home" (32). As a parent, he has not been able to continue his life in the woods, isolated and in tune with nature but not used to the ways of people: "We—Lucy and me—the girls—we aren't used to living by the side of people. I guess that's it. Lucy thought the girls ought, well, to meet—you know—though neither Angela nor Eleanor seems to care about that" (192).

Now in a town, Omensetter is forced out into the company of people and their words; he has begun his descent into knowledge, into self-consciousness; and the awareness of this new responsibility sinks him to the bottom—following the path of the stones that he "teases" into temporary weightlessness. Words, particularly those from Furber (symbolized by the sinkers thrown at Omensetter's hat floating down the river), have their effect on him. He comes to see himself as less than sufficient, less than whole, less than "lucky." Henry Pimber notices the change that takes place in Omensetter: "If Brackett Omensetter had ever had the secret of how to live, he hadn't known it. Now the difference was—he knew. Everyone at last had managed to tell him, and now like everybody else he was wondering what it was. Like everybody else" (63). Omensetter seeks Furber's advice about what to do regarding Pimber's body swinging from the tree limb, and Lucy Pimber insists that the doctor be called to treat her sick baby rather than relying on her husband's legendary (and heretofore taken-for-granted) healing powers. Omensetter begins to petrify like all the others in Gilean and like the others risks the danger of "splashing under" (118). Like Furber, he initiates the building of a walled-in garden of the self: "No miracle, a man with a man's mask and a man's wall" (63).

The Garden and the Tree

I have stated that *Omensetter's Luck* is, at its root, the positing of one great idea, the tension between animal and mineral, humanity and the world of things, being and not being, good and evil, innocence and knowledge, reason and feeling, mind and body. In other words, the novel is a working out of the basic metaphor of art and culture: the myth of Adam and Eve and the Garden.[21]

This dialectic or oppositional method of exploring primal conflicts of the sort mentioned above—conflicts that have been with us since the beginning—is centered on a kind of geometric framework that calls to mind some of the writing of Gertrude Stein and John Fowles (who overtly and heavily borrows in this regard from Jung's theories of the self). Stein's *Q.E.D.* delineates three psychological types that relate to each other in a geometric pattern. A kind of revolving or cyclic triangularity through a three-year round of events highlights the contests of two lesbians for the love of the third member of a homosexual triangle, the dominant woman and the love object of the other two. This novella is a careful exposition of the psychological cores (that Stein considers present from birth in all people and that surfaces with time and/or intense scrutiny) of the three characters based on their conversations and interactions—very little traditional background information emerges. The often obsessive use of triangulation merely ties together the fragments of personality that can be revealed in character development through language—language that probes every cranny in the triangular relationships and then brings the reader back to a beginning point.[22] In *Tender Buttons* Stein resorts to a kind of circular pattern that Allegra Stewart has called a mandala structure. Stewart's Jungian interpretation of *Tender Buttons* is an attempt to link its surface arrangement of character with substructures that approximate a Gertrude Stein brand of the collective unconscious.[23]

I have mentioned already that John Fowles, in *The Ebony Tower,* crafts his allegory of being and art out of characters arranged in a four-quadrant circle system based on the Jungian *quaternion.* Unlike the Stein and Gass works, Fowles's text refers directly to Jung. The quadrilateral interlacing of character in *The Ebony Tower* is strikingly similar to the way characters develop in *Omensetter's Luck.* The Fowles piece, like the Gass work, is a parody or a reworking of a worn-out convention: *The Ebony Tower* reworks the medieval lay, while Gass takes the American folk legend as his underlying foundation. Like many writers of the midtwentieth century, Fowles and Gass seem to have felt the need to revitalize conventional forms by expansion or exaggeration: in the case of these two, the intensification takes the form of a highly stylized probing of deeper, universal concepts by means of a meticulously erected, (geometric) allegorical armature that reminds me of one of those designs made by stretching string between many pairs of small nails. The four characters in the Fowles novella stand for four elements of a mandala partly composed of Jung's "Moses *Quaternio.*" This mandala is based on Gnostic Christian theology and medieval Hermetism (zodiacal and alchemical lore) and partly made up of the emblems of the four triplicities of the zodiac.[24] Jung's system features Moses as culture hero, Zipporah as higher mother, the Lower Adam as prelapsarian or "somatic" man, and Eve as a kind of earth mother, and exemplifies the various "syzygies" of diametrical meshings and separations that expand the basic fourfold structure.[25] Jung's scheme includes a higher Jethro, the "great wise one" (like Pike in *Omensetter's Luck*), the embodiment of the archetype of the "spirit in myth and folklore," and a lower Jethro (like Gass's Jethro), the "heathen priest and stranger . . . with a magical and nefarious significance.[26]

Foisting an extratextual system of explanation upon a work is dangerous. There is no overt call from the text of *Omensetter's Luck* to justify a
Jungian reading. Gass discusses Jung in one of his essays (*WWW,* 246),
but makes no mention of these theories in his fiction. Therefore, I refer to
Jung's *quaternion* model of the self only as a coincidence, or, as I have stated
earlier, as a mutual tapping of some hidden stream that appears to feed the
wells of both writers. The coincidences are evident, however, and, as in the
case of Gertrude Stein, more than likely reflect an interest (on the part of all
three) in basic psychological types and the symbolic or allegorical possibilities presented by those types.

If Jung used Hermetic lore for his circular structures and syzygies, Gass
sticks to the biblical figures of the Garden, Adam and Eve, and God and
Satan for his. Omensetter and Furber make up the main axial antagonism;
this relationship is heightened and diversified by a series of lesser oppositions:
Henry–Lucy Pimber, Omensetter–Pimber, Furber–Tott, Furber–Lucy
Omensetter, Furber–Pike, Pike–Omensetter, Lucy Pimber–Lucy
Omensetter. All these duos interconnect and link with the archetype of the
Garden, the sacred inside ground opposed to the profane outside, the inno-
cent, secure interior set against the chaotic outside of the experiential world.

We have seen that Furber lives behind the walls of the church garden and
behind his barricade of words. The church garden is also, of course, the cemetery; Furber thus inhabits a graveyard. His isolation from the general flow of
life in his parish makes him, particularly in comparison to the overflowing
love and naturalness of Omensetter, a figure of stony lifelessness. His garden
has been closed off for a long time: "the lock was rusted now and the double
gates were bound" (64). His words serve to reinforce mentally his physical
separateness: he spends himself, like Tott, his doddering counterpart, weaving webs of protective verbiage, "charming himself with his rhetoric like a
snake playing the flute" (74). But his solitude and his stream of words also
lead him to glimpse the truth; although he deceives others, he reveals little
self-deception. He ruminates at great length about the truth of the Fall and
the Garden and the Tree of Knowledge: "Men, like all things, resist their essence, and seek the sweet oblivion of the animal—a rest from themselves
that's but an easy counterfeit of death . . . Yet when Adam disobeyed, he lit
this sun in our heads. Now, like the slowest worm, we sense; but like the
mightiest god, we *know*" (174–75).

Furber's knowledge, the knowledge of good and evil symbolized by the
tree, leads him into a logical pattern, a fiction about the perplexing,
attractive-repulsive nature of Omensetter: "For whatever Omensetter does
he does without desire in the ordinary sense, with a kind of abandon, a stony

mindlessness that makes me always think of Eden . . . And this of course is the clue, for more than any man I've ever known, Omensetter seems beyond the reach of God. He's truly out of touch . . . Sins's nothing but exile. It occurs when God withdraws . . . Yet Omensetter does not seem to be. He does not seem. Seem . . . And what shall we conclude from all this then? / We must conclude he is the worst. / He is the worst. / Therefore" (126). This sinister syllogism at first glance has the appearance of error, as purely an attempt by its perpetrator to subvert the standing of a rival whose innocence has made the maligning party appear evil—and that surely is part of the matter. It is, after all, Omensetter's healing luck in the form of a folk remedy—a beet poultice—not Furber's prayers based on the systemized perception called theology or Doc Orcutt's perceptual construct called science, that has saved Pimber from tetanus. The minister and the doctor have been shown up by legend, the shaman, the legendary nature healer.

Furber is right, however, to find evil in what the people of his church have found so attractive—the attempt to turn their backs on their own views of the world and the ordering of it into human terms and to sink back into the life of a "cat in a chair," the purely physical existence of "sense" that Eden stands for. Sin is indeed where God is not because God is where human beings are; human beings are both "worms" in sensation and "gods" in knowledge. Prelapsarian Adam in his purity, like Omensetter, is "lower Adam," a monster, not human; but Satan, like Furber, is equally monstrous because he is walled away from humanity.

The central confrontation of the novel is that between Adam-Omensetter and Satan-Furber, but other lines of syzygy run off this opposition, and it is in these minor alignments that the geometric substructure of psychological type appears. Pimber and Omensetter carry on a relationship that is as charged with meaning and that develops the Garden archetype as fully as any other. Pimber is a pale copy of Furber; he lacks the latter's verbal (and therefore intellectually redemptive) power. He desires, nevertheless, the same somatic freedom of Eden that Furber in his own way also seeks. Pimber, like Furber, is walled in, but not by words; his prison is what Gass has called in an essay "working consciousness," a kind of stifling routinism, a dumb, unimaginative life (*FFL*, 269). His first full look at Omensetter is (literally) through a screen (door); once he removes the screen, the filter, from the overpowering phenomenon of the man, he falls under the power of the luck.

Pimber had wanted to be an Adam; like Adam, he is a namer and can name the trees (55). In imitating Omensetter, he wants to go beyond naming, beyond knowing. "Naming is knowing" (107), says Furber; Gass explains what Pimber really wants: he wants what all of us want at times, to "feel at home in our body, to sense the true *nostos* of it, . . . to have it move to our will so smoothly we seem will-less altogether" (*FFL*, 261). He has the unwanted but unshakable responsibility of a god, a god to an Adam renting his "garden," his structure: "Had he thought they were playing at Adam and Eve: three children and a dog? *Paradise by Riverside* . . . Exorbitantly leased from Mr. Henry God, a lesser demon." (58). Henry Pimber wants to go beyond the fallen Adam who knows and who is therefore responsible. He wants to be inhuman. To be Omensetter, for Pimber, is to be inhuman: "Not Adam but inhuman. Was that why he loved him, Henry wondered" (58). Pimber's equation of luck with stepping out of his humanity, of course, is suicidal. Thus, Pimber's luck is misfortune; he falls, like the fox in the well, further into his mundane life. In a moment of revelation, he sees the fox as his alternate self, his real self, the Henry Pimber that is a prisoner of his circumstances: "What an awful thing: to have the earth open to swallow you almost the moment you took the hen in your jaws and to die in a tube" (39). To put an end to Omensetter's curious unconcern for the fox and to kill the "Pimber down the well" self ("Murder would also be suicide" [40]), he shoots the fox to put it out of its pain; a fragment of the shotgun charge wounds Pimber and the infected wound produces lockjaw. Omensetter cures him and makes him his disciple: "Henry was newborn in that waltzing body now" (47).

Pimber wants not to climb the tree of human perception and knowledge as does the child who tells Tott that he lives in a tree, "a high tree" that "goes way up into the air and you can see clean to Columbus" (14), or as he does himself when he follows Omensetter up into the tree to "see" (59). Instead, he wants to become a part of the tree of unmixed being (the Omensetter that is as "inhuman as a tree" [58]), the tree of unconscious life; he wants to hang in it like a leaf. He plans on a "leave taking" (63). In other words, he seeks the only alternative, death.

These thoughts reveal how Pimber, in addition to his association with Omensetter, shares a syzygy with Furber, a relationship that produces yet another ligament, another line in the geometry of the story. In his attempt to imitate Omensetter directly, Pimber furnishes an opposite to Furber in that both try to re-create Omensetter, but Pimber by action attempts a union with the phenomenon. Furber shields himself from the painful-to-behold Omensetter by creating a fiction of the man, a symbol without the body: he develops a word-induced vision of Omensetter and gives the real man a new name, dubs his "luck" magic, and seeks to pervert his place in the society of the town. The latter method is much safer; a fictionalized Omensetter is much easier to deal with. The link between Pimber and the parson emphasizes the protection afforded by language and its ability to modify a reality that is impossible to reach. Pimber continues to think and to analyze, but is not able to turn his ideal into a fiction; neither is he able to accept the "real" Omensetter, the Omensetter who is changing before his eyes into a man just like other men (63). He notices that Omensetter has begun to clean his fingernails, has given in to respectability, has lost his wildness. As his model slips from inhumanity into humanity, Pimber himself falls back into his old "stone" self, the opposite of his "tree" self, a self filled with "sudden rushes of unnaturally sharp, inhuman vision in which all things were dazzling, glorious, and terrifying," in which he thinks he "saw . . . as Omensetter saw, except for painful beauty" (57).

Redemption

The suicidal Pimber, juxtaposed to the survivalist Furber, magnifies the latter's "change of heart" and eventual redemption. Although Furber has the same appetite for the gates of the Garden that Pimber has, the diabolical cleric wallows in "prejudice of heart" and "artifice of mind" to block out and controvert "the world as the world is really." His rhetorical reconstitution of naked reality, although initially walling out human warmth and love and substituting symbols of things for the things themselves ("for him they were the thing, the actual opera, itself" [163]), leads him at last to valuable insight regarding his condition: he sees the power and the authenticity of his bellowing "at the foot of the tree." His verbal re-creation of a world, his self-protective lying, his nose thumbing at the Omensetter "nature legend," and his thorough knowledge of the theology of Eden force him to see his limits clearly. He understands that the exact opposite of innocence (unconditional love) is unrelenting perception and that language is the main vehicle of that perception. He knows that seeing through animal eyes, after the fashion of Omensetter, is no longer possible for us. Seeing through human eyes necessarily involves consciousness and meaning. Although Pimber, too, knows the pain of perception, the "painful beauty" (57) that prohibits his seeing as Omensetter sees, he persists in his "inhuman vision" (57) of escaping his dreary life, the life of the fox caught in the well. Of course the only way to remedy the fox's plight is to kill it.

Furber, however, rejects suicide, preferring to wrestle against the dream of innocence, even against divinity. In doing so, he dignifies his Satanic position, and relishes his ejection from the Garden and even his opposition to the God that he preaches about: "So then it is the Devil, of course, the sly old snake, who is holiest . . . think of that. He fell, he was The Fall itself, the suicidal star; but he fell at the end of a fine elastic" (74–75). Furber finds in this path the alternative to suicide; he creates a world opposite to reality, opposite to Eden, and even opposite to God. He creates a world with words and then allows God, always present at the other end of the elastic, to come in and inhabit this world. Because he is master of his own territory, master of language, "the wondrous watchman," he "sees without blinking" because "thought lies on the other side of that thin lid" (175). And rigorous dialectic dictates that the opposite, the other side, must be struggled against and sought fervently at the same time in order to have a proper balance between the two points of a syzygy: God seeks himself in man just as man seeks himself in God.

Strength, in other words, comes from resistance, and Furber can imagine that even God needs resistance from man in order to get the proper dynamic tension, the necessary "exercise" to combat "softening." Thus, when, at the death of Pimber, Omensetter comes to Furber and asks for his help as a friend, Furber sees himself, in the role of Satan ("the Opposer"—as the name *Satan* translates), as in need of the chief quality that his opponent stands for—unconditional and uncritical love: "A friend, eh? a friend, a friend . . . What a godforsaken soul I have. Ba—Brackett—what a shit I am" (191). Furber, who had made up a word-centered being, a fiction called Backett Omensetter, just as he had made up a being called God out of words that substituted for real qualities, now, with full comprehension, reverses the process: "Backett" is transformed into "Brackett"; Omensetter's luck becomes what it has really been all along—Omensetter's love, childish and untrammeled, but pure. And "God was coming true" for him, "coming slowly to light like a message in lemon . . . Wasn't it what he'd always wanted— God to exist?" (208). Unlike Pimber, whose flesh has become a symbol, an actual body hanging on a limb, a leaf on the tree of being, Furber's symbols have become flesh; in theological terms, the *logoi spermatikoi* have reached incarnation. If Omensetter's acquisition of human perception has brought him doubt and insecurity, Furber's move along the axis of syzygy from the other end toward love has opened for him the realm of love; he has become in his controlled way a little like Omensetter: "Furber's body shook with the spasms of uncontrollable laughter, his mouth gaped and his chest heaved as if he were Brackett Omensetter himself in the deep bend of his luck" (235).

William Gass has said that he is not good at making plots in the traditional sense. He compensates for this lack of ability in *Omensetter's Luck* by building a complex superstructure upon the base of a standard American legend. Driving rhythm and delicate interplay of folk and popular songs of the late nineteenth century undergird and bind the elements of what substitutes for plot. Of course, the telling of the legend in this whimsical, metafictional way more than makes up for plot originality, and the musicality and meta-phorical deployment of the characters, allegorical in their symbolic opposi-tion to their various counterparts, burn the images of the principal names and their lilting speeches into our minds as few conventional characterizations can. And, above all else, the high degree of craftsmanship and complexity of form leave in the mind of the reader the lesson of the central image, again, a well-known one to be sure, the happy error of falling into human perception that carries with it not only the longing of the "saddest animal" (214) but also the possibility of redemption. The novel is a restatement of Gass's central lit-erary precept: that language is both bondage and freedom. The novelist, "if he is any good, will keep us kindly imprisoned in his language" (*FFL*, 8) and will lead us at the same time to imagine a contrary world that will allow na-ture to live with us on our own terms and permit us to live in it. Gass contin-ues this theme (the interplay of world and word) in his next work, *In the Heart of the Heart of the Country,* a collection of short stories.

Chapter Three

In the Heart of the Heart of the Country: "An Uneasy Peace of Equal Powers"

Two years separated the publication of *Omensetter's Luck* from that of *In the Heart of the Heart of the Country,* a collection of short fiction that reached bookstore and library shelves in 1968. Despite the depth, cohesion, and verbal brilliance of the novel, it is this book of short stories that has secured a place for William Gass in the history of modern literature. Two of these pieces, "The Pedersen Kid" and "The Order of Insects," along with the work of Barth, Barthelme, Coover, and Elkin, frequently find their way into anthologies of current experimental fiction.[1]

Although each story is presented as a distinct entity, a strong thread runs through them all, tying them together into variations on the familiar Gass theme, established in *Omensetter's Luck*: the revelation afforded by an awareness of the oppositional nature of the world, particularly the dichotomy between words and reality, between engagement with and aesthetic estrangement from people, animals, and objects. The narrators of these stories are offspring or subspecies of Jethro Furber: they are alienated; they peer at their surroundings through screens made of language; they hide behind windows and doors and look out at things. The powerful language that dominates this work is what we have come to expect from Gass: it is rhythmic, alliterative, and laden with striking images; it pulls our attention away from the telling of the tales and into its own thick mix, a vortex that is every bit as entertaining as the movement of the narrative.

"The Pedersen Kid"

The first story, in length approximating a novella, is a parody of a conventional form: the detective story. It also makes use of the ancient plot device of a journey, even referred to here as a knightly quest. A boy, nearly frozen to death, is found in the barn of the Segren family by the Segren's hired hand,

Hans. Hans succeeds in bringing Stevie Pedersen, a kid from a farm some distance away, back to life by rubbing him with snow and pouring liquor down his throat. As the boy gradually warms and regains consciousness, he tells Hans that an armed intruder wearing yellow gloves has killed his parents and thrown their bodies into the cellar. Throughout the revival of the Pedersen boy, Jorge Segren, the adolescent narrator, relates anecdotes and reveals details that present his life as a grim ordeal of loveless existence: his father is a vicious and abusive drunk; and his mother, submissive to her husband and his outrages and resigned to exist at the level of a housework automaton, has neither the courage nor the love necessary to be a proper mother to her son. Hans, who occasionally shows some slight interest in Jorge, is for most of the time just an extension of his employer, Jorge's Pa, cruel and self-absorbed. Hans, Pa, and Jorge set out in the bitter cold to investigate the reported murder; Jorge begins the journey seeing himself as a crusader bent on doing praiseworthy deeds,[2] but Pa and Hans go in order to engage in a kind of contest of wills, a mutual punishment for past rancor brought to life again in an altercation over the bottle of liquor used in the resuscitation of the Pedersen kid. The story reaches an indeterminate ending when the three arrive at the Pedersen place: Pa is somehow shot, Hans runs away, and Jorge is left alone in the cold house with a burning, deranged mind (79).

Reflecting Gass's belief that fiction is not as much an act of mimesis as an art of configuration, the movement of the story relies on syzygy or axial tension between apparent opposites—counterpoised characters and images (as in *Omensetter's Luck*). Time sets the first polar relationship: spring counters and delineates winter. Jorge thinks often of the return of warmer weather, and with it the melting of the snow, the sun-induced liquefaction of solid ice (11), the time when, had the Pedersen kid not been rescued from the cold and brought into the heat of the kitchen, his soft, curled-up body, like a fetus, would be found, like a black stone in a field exposed suddenly by melting snow (12). Like the black stone discovered in a field at Mecca, the imagined body of the kid, having acquired the status of something sacred, affords Jorge a moment of revelation about the freedom and rest to be found in petrified nonbeing. He imagines himself in the place of the Pedersen kid, imagines what it must feel like to slip slowly into the sleeplike coma of hypothermia, to become stony and black like the coals in the heater in his mother's kitchen, to achieve a kind of hallucinated warmth in freezing. His uncovering as the snow melts in the spring would bring the revelation of his petrification (13). "Uncovering," a possible translation of the Greek *apoka-lupsis* (apocalypse), can mean the end, the separation of the two great elements of the struggle of being, evil and good, body and soul, and by analogy, in this case, winter's cold and spring's heat. The end of winter brings the end of the struggle with snow, and the black stone, which balances the white petrification of ice, calls to mind again the struggle between the light-tinted angel and the dark Satan in Blake's pictorial rendering of the verses from Apocalypse (20:1–3). The chaining of Satan brings not only unadulterated goodness but also the end of the world for human beings, mortal middles in the dialectical attenuation between eternal poles. Even Hans, whom Jorge calls "a savior" (21), and who, like a roughneck priest, lays his large hands on the frozen body of the Pedersen boy and pours a foul, yet warming, communion indelicately into his mouth while he rolls him in dough and kneads him like communion bread—even Hans is held by time and cannot thaw out the kid ahead of schedule. Victims of the cold have to be thawed slowly, maintains Jorge: "He's got to thaw slow. You ought to know that" (9).

Snow, paradoxically, when rubbed on frostbite, warms. Just as winter, given time, metamorphoses into spring, so snow, given the time of a journey or a story, can become warm. The Pedersen kid in his journey through a frozen world has found, not the black petrification that is death, but the heat of the black stove in the kitchen, the same image of black life in the middle of white death that wells up inside Jorge as he trudges through the snowstorm (ritually repeating the journey of the kid) toward the Pedersen farm. He thinks of the black stone with its black soot and the cherry-red fire and the black kettle with the hissing white steam (43). White, the white of steam (snow juxtaposed to intense heat from the black coal), now brings life, foreshadowing Jorge's joyful final "burning" as he freezes to death in the last scene. This constant tightening and loosening of the vincula between cold/white and heat/black provides the narrative platform for the story, paving the way for the development of characters and for the moment of tense revelation at the end.

Both plot and character, like the prevailing images of the story (heat–cold, black–white, winter–spring, and so forth), are indeterminate. Matching these bipolar extensions, the plot and the characters oscillate between one justifiable interpretation and another. This story is Gass's most mimetically conceived; it was supposed to follow a standard linear format, and the speech of Jorge was intended to conform to that of a child.[3] Regardless of the author's reservations about too tight and commonplace a structure, the movement of the piece does not by any means merely waltz along in standard fashion. Beneath the thin glaze of realism (a graphically imagined setting, strong fashioning of character, a suspense-structured plot based on the journey motif, and an expectation in the reader's mind, fostered by traditional unravelings of mysteries that supposedly reveal and reinforce sym-

bolism), stands a substructure of hesitation and inconclusiveness that
makes the dense language appear to be all there is at the center. Because the
narrator finds no answer to the mystery and the story ends with his unbalanced inner monologue, the outcomes that have been hinted at become
suddenly unimportant and opaque.

The expectations created by the plot line are controverted by the possible
madness of Jorge: the fiction, the "something" that came through the snow
with the Pedersen kid and the something that Hans brought to life with his
rubbing, has taken on a life of its own and may no longer match the given set
of happenings. If the killer in the yellow gloves and green coat has killed the
Pedersens, where are the bodies? Instead of the promised corpses in the cellar,
Jorge has found a place to dream, perhaps to die. The killer is never seen, only
suggested; and why does he spare Jorge and kill Pa? Could Jorge have killed
Pa? After all, the boy has a gun and imagines killing everybody and even relishes their deaths. Is Hans killed, too, or does he run away? Either way, Hans
and Pa exit the hallucinated thoughts of Jorge and confirm the latter's desire:
to be free of adult abuse and oppression. He would also be left alone to freeze
to death; no Hans would rescue him by rubbing as he had the kid. What finally happens to Ma, Hans, Little Hans, the Pedersens, and Stevie remains
hidden.[4] The suspense that accrues with the movement of the story remains
unresolved. The promise that plot makes is not kept; the story turns against
itself, leaving the narrator adrift in a twisted and beautiful solipsism.

The characters are drawn together by the dominant metaphor of the story,
the inner core of warmth contrasted starkly with the terrible outside world of
cold. The bottle symbolizes the warmth and life of spring, and its ritual use
unifies characters otherwise skewed out along their respective lines of hatred
and divergence of purpose.

The central conflict is that of Jorge against his environment. Jorge's life
with his family and Hans sets up the ritual journey to self-liberation typical of
conventional stories of innocence and maturity. The boy's need and his efforts
to develop independence are brought into intense relief by his hatred of his
father; again, this antagonism is universal in father-son pairings. But rarely
do fathers reach the degree of despicability of Pa, and with it, the worthiness
of the death that awaits him at the end of the story. He is more than capable
of violence and he can do great physical damage to his family—as the scar on
Ma's face attests. He has nothing but curses and insults for his son; sitting in
the sleigh wrapped in a blanket, he makes Jorge dig into the snow to retrieve
the dropped bottle of booze and is more concerned about the shivering of his
horse than his own son's discomfort (40).

Even worse than Pa's constant ill treatment of Jorge is his refusal to recognize that his son is moving toward adulthood. Searching for Pa's lost bottle, Jorge asks if Pa will let him have a drink if the bottle is found (38). The conversation that follows is a dialogue of exclusion from, rather than an initiation into, manhood: "Ain't you growed up—a man—since yesterday! I've had a few, Pa. Ha. Of what, hey? Hear that, Hans? He's had a few" (38). It is here that the symbol of the bottle reaches its apex of meaning.

If the journey to the Pedersen's farm is a pilgrimage, a knight's quest, Pa's liquor bottle functions as the grail. The ritual of the cup, in archaic religions as well as in orthodox Christianity, has liturgically nourished the hope of life in the midst of death, spring as opposed to winter, regeneration in the face of decomposition, eternal order out of ephemeral chaos. Simultaneously freezing to death and having visions of warm fires and springtime, Jorge imagines that his father, dead now, comes to "haunt" him; Pa's ghost tries to remind him that the bottle was only for winter, meaning a man-made warmth, a cozy artifact, a symbol of life in the dead time of bitter cold. Pa says that the bottle makes spring come for him just as the mysterious killer in the yellow gloves makes spring come for Jorge (74). Although Jorge acknowledges that Pa drinks only in winter (74), he still associates Pa's brutality and repression, indeed Pa himself, with the bottle: "You're no man now. Your bottle's broken in the snow" (74). "No man" rhymes with "snow man"; Pa's body coalesces with his counterpart, the snowman in the Pedersens' yard; he has no bottle, no warmth at the core; he has been petrified by death and covered by the falling snow (78). Pa's ghost, however, keeps on talking to Jorge and at last brings up the pictures in Hans's girlie books, photographs of big-breasted girls with nipples like the bottoms of brown bottles (74), brown nipples and bottles now amalgamating alcohol with the element of sexual maturity.

Jorge wants to reach manhood, but even though Hans has shown him some pictures of naked girls, the deep rite of initiation, in the Dionysian form of alcoholic drink, is denied him. What makes matters worse is that his rival, the Pedersen kid, *has* been given the liquid warmth from Pa's bottle to rekindle his life center; and although this use is medicinal in the physical sense, Jorge's psychological need for metaphysical or ritual inclusion in the warmth of manhood is just as great; he, too, is frozen—frozen out of the love that he must have to be fully alive. Just as Jethro Furber envies his counterpart Omensetter for the latter's capacity to love and be loved, so Jorge chafes at the attention his family gives the Pedersen kid. In addition to being given alcohol, the kid is warmed, talked about, worried over, ritually consumed (compared to ham and the makings of bread)—in other words, made totally a part of the warm kitchen—and then placed in Hans's warm bed. Ma, who never takes notice of Jorge except to scold him, even plans to make biscuits and coffee for the Pedersens who are thought to be on the way to see their son.

But also like Furber, Jorge overcomes his initial antipathy for his rival and derives pleasure from contemplating the similarities between them; Jorge seems to glory in their "exchange," for in a moment of deep insight, he realizes that both boys really had, in their battles with the mounting snow and the frozen countryside, done great deeds. Both had become free of parental control, had come out of the cold and had found warmth; both had arrived at new, unfamiliar domains (73) of adult independence, of spring (symbolized by the killer in green and gold). The sun (gold) and the returning vegetation (green) "rot" the snow and kill the snowmen (40). The sun of spring is like a discharge from a gun: in Jorge's mind, it flashes out of Pa's gun barrel like a bullet (78). And among the sun's victims are the snowmen, also the "no men," the frozen corpses of parents.

As in *Omensetter's Luck,* Gass makes use of pairs of doubles to delineate character and enhance the ideas that lie behind his character development. The result is a balanced allegory of being and artistic creation. Pa and Hans are double images of rough nastiness, a pair of conventional villains whose foul treatment of the child-narrator builds up in the reader's mind a need for justice, a justification for rejoicing when icy death takes them. Likewise, Jorge and the Pedersen kid make up the double image of the protagonist in search of his place in a hostile environment. There are lesser pairings, such as the two farm houses, Horse Simon and the Pedersen horse, that assist the configural movement of the story, and, in the case of Big Hans from the Segren farm and Little Hans Pedersen, counterparts that seem to have no narrative function. But all these conjunctions work to set up the "this" and the "other" development that is a hallmark of Gass's fiction.

In "The Pedersen Kid," the allegorical struggle of cold against warmth, winter against spring, adult against child, world against self, or any of the other conflicts implied by an inside-outside antithesis marks out the limits of being that again calls to mind Yeats's gyres and the yin-yang circle. In these circular oppositions, always exists, at the moment of extreme difference, a tiny particle of likeness, a seed of commonality or affinity that grows and allows for the eventual reversal of the opposites, an "exchange" or oscillation between extremes that is at the heart of ontology. The extreme limit of cold seems to bring with it the potential for warmth. It is at the moment when cold drives Jorge into craziness, when he points the gun at Pa and Hans and threatens to kill them, that Pa warms up just a little to Jorge, whose person and comfort he has heretofore ignored. Pa invites Jorge to have some coffee—a black drink to match the black heat of Ma's stove (52). Of course this tiny breach in Pa's customary cruelty is made even smaller by a stinging blow to the face that he has just given Jorge. Hans, in the same way, eases the ligament of hate that joins him to Pa by offering (instead of being ordered) to let Pa ride the only horse back home when the trace breaks. Pa is surprised at this generosity. Jorge realizes that there is an element of goodness in the bitter cold. The "good in cold" (41) is dramatized when the cold again drives Jorge into himself, into his imaginary spring based on an actual spring when he and Hans had been on good terms, and Hans had been like an older brother to him, a kind of hero for him to emulate. Then Hans had let Jorge help him with chores, had let him see the girlie magazines, and had told the boy war stories (70–71). Big Hans, unlike Stevie Pedersen's brother, Little Hans, has in his hands the power to bring warmth and life to a cold child just as he does by massaging the cold Stevie with snow, bringing to bear the paradoxically healing goodness from an otherwise lethal snow.

The intensity of the cold and the rising accumulation of snow on the land that lies between the Segren's place and the Pedersen's farm make the journey to solve the mystery of the killer in green, yellow, and black a true ordeal. The extreme discomfort of the cold trek magnifies the need for escape into its opposite: arrival at a warm spot. Again there is the paradox of Jorge's act of leaving his house, a place of physical warmth, where the kid is revived near Ma's hot stove and is put to bed in Hans's warm bed, but a place that Jorge has found intolerably cold in other than physical ways, to journey to a house where he freezes to death outwardly but burns with joy inside and feels the way one is supposed to feel in church (79). Again, this goodness embedded in the cold is symbolized by the black coals of the Pedersens' furnace (64). Jorge keeps making fires in the fireplace and those fires continue to turn gray and go out, thus leaving the boy between the black of the stove in his dreams of home and the white snow mounting up outside, in the gray zone between life and death.

The synthesis or amalgam of all these oppositions is the killer, a color configuration of Hans and Pa, spring and winter, heat and cold. The killer's green mackinaw stands for Jorge's family, personified negatively by Pa Segren, whose surname is a disguised form of sea green or seed green. Jorge, looking at his father in bed under the covers, compares the man's head to a "dandelion gone to seed" (4). As Pa's body lies under the mounting snow in the Pedersens' yard, his dry crack of a mouth finally silenced, Jorge thinks of spring in terms of a dandelion-covered meadow where the ground was cracked, where dandelions went to seed, and where as a small child he had "shot" Pa with his broomstick gun. In the frozen house, Jorge imagines himself as he will be found in the spring, hanging in a cocoon (66); he then notices the green wallpaper. He suddenly realizes the connection between his name, his possible bright future as a free adult and a propagator of his lineage, Pa's snowman corpse with his gun in an upright, phallic position, and the mysterious killer. He laughs at the green flowerpot design on the wallpaper and then sees the stranger's footprints on the porch (66–67). Pa's hair is compared to glistening snow, Pa himself to a snowman, and the killer to a being that was at home in the snow like a fish in a lake (72).

Pa Segren is clearly an element of the killer. But since Pa is compared metaphorically to a dandelion, with associations of spring, greenness, and seeds, Jorge senses that the winter figure, the killer, is both a liberator from and a perpetuation of the bondage of his father. The kid, Jorge's syzygy, finds warmth in being a Pedersen in the Segren house just as Jorge glories in being a Segren in the Pedersen house. The killer, partly symbolic of the deadness of winter, dramatizes the germinal good found in extremes, in cold or in heat or in any aspect of the world around us. The killer not only has killed the parents but also has given life and made redemption possible by forcing awareness of being: "The kid and me, we'd done brave things well worth remembering" (79).

If the green coat suggests Pa's frozen malignancy with its seed of regeneration in his son, the yellow gloves stretch a line to Hans, called "yellow Hans" (51). As has been stated, the hands of yellow Hans, by rubbing, by frictional heat, transform snow into a life-giving material. The color yellow, together with the mention of heat, suggests the sun. The sun, of course, draws near the earth once again in the spring, melting and warming, restoring the proper climate for vegetal rebirth. The heat in the sunlike hands of Hans leads to the final color in the configural unity of the killer, the black hat. The black hat, like the black coal that warms, the black stone of the kid's corpse potentially found in the spring, and the black horse on which the killer rides, means warmth, black warmth—the opposite of white cold. Hans is yellow because he runs away—he escapes becoming a snowman corpse in the yard. And sunlight brightly burns on the escape route that Jorge plans (78). He sees a dark shadow moving out in the snow ahead of him; the stranger is leaving (78). The figure with the green coat, black hat, and yellow hands—the composite of father, family, sun, redemption, and warmth—represents the reciprocal, dialectical nature of being; being is both death and life at once.

"Mrs. Mean"

Like "The Pedersen Kid," and, for that matter, all the pieces in *In the Heart of the Heart of the Country,* this story expresses a chain linking of dialectical extensions. It also manifests a familiar philosophical underpinning and serves as a fertile ground for making inferences about fictional theory and technique. The ontological hub of "Mrs. Mean" is the archaic, pre-Socratic idea that all things are made up of four primary elements—fire, earth, air, and water—that combine and disassociate by means of the opposing forces of harmony and strife. The Pluralists of the fifth century B.C., particularly Empedocles, considered the fusion and separation of these parts to be fundamental in the cyclic differentiation into form and reversion to chaos that all things must undergo.

The story begins with a disquisition on naming, essence, and "the grandeur of Being" (80). The narrator, observing a woman and her family from his porch shaded by large trees, reminds us of Jethro Furber. He watches other people in the act of going through the natural events of their family life; and, since he cannot become a part of the scene before him even though he finds certain aspects of it attractive, he creates a fiction about it, making up characters to match the real people before him. The name that he gives the woman that attracts his attention is not her real name, which he does not know, but one that he has contrived for the purpose of interpreting for himself her existence (80). This name, like the fictional label "Backett" that Furber gives Omensetter, is obviously abstract, suggesting "the glassy essence, the grotesquerie of Type" (80) like a character from a comedy of manners (like those of Restoration playwright William Congreve), shallow, summarizing categories of being. This name abstracts from particulars, creating a consensus of details that elevates its object to the formality of being relieved from the baggage of reality. In other words, the name "Mrs. Mean," at least for the narrator, makes the untouchable woman across the way a character of fiction who is only suggested by the reality of life behind the name. The narrator, unable really to know the "Means," dehumanizes them by reducing them to fictional centers of imagination; and like Furber, this narrator must see such dehumanized people as evil and mean, like Backett Omensetter the legend, as contrasted with Brackett Omensetter the man. The narrator's wife does her neighbor the same disservice; the fact that she prefers to create more positive characters in her fiction is nonetheless just as dehumanizing.

Fire is the first Empedoclean component of being, and heat and fire characterize the big-breasted, sun-drenched woman who hobbles about on her treeless—thus always open to the sun—lawn. Opposing the narrator-voyeur who feels that he has, in his motionless fabrication and false character stamping, become like an idle god, Mrs. Mean defies any effort to make her stop long enough to fall into easy characterization. She "burns" before him (88). Mrs. Mean, in the eyes of the narrator, is like a fire alarm (89). She is in constant motion, weeding and clipping her perfect lawn, raking and planting, trying to keep her children from ruining her grass. Her eyes "blaze" with what the narrator perceives as a fiery divinity (88–89). The imagery of heat in these lines enlivens the woman's perceived persona, hammering it (in the narrator's mind) into an image of animalistic sexuality: "She revolves her backside carefully against a tree" (88).

In order to deal with this raw sensuality, the narrator, who cannot dare to let his transcendental idleness suffer such inordinate disruption, creates an artificial religious narrowness to contain it. The narrator has seen signs for sale that say "Eternity Tomorrow"; Mr. Mean buys one of these signs and nails it on his garage door. The narrator, eschewing his wife's prosaic interpretation of these words (that it is merely a reminder to drive safely), converts this sign into a range of reasons for the Means's supposed guilt-ridden and fanatic suppression of the sensual. The Means, according to his private fictions, must be coldhearted Calvinists who live by impossibly strict sexual standards. Just as Furber condemns Omensetter on religious grounds (for not being formally religious), the narrator here denigrates the Means' supposed excessive religious structure, finding therein a counterweight for his libidinous fantasies about Mrs. Mean.

The narrator often rejects his wife's more positive views of the Means, particularly in the case of Mrs. Mean, who appears to her to be an efficient housewife, whose home "is always cool and dry and airy" (105). He sets his own negative trilogy of archaic ontological attributes against those (in their positive state) offered by his wife. For him, the Mean house is airless, with its windows always closed, no breeze, damp walls, and sweating toilets (104). To his wife's description, a description that involves the absence of heat and moisture, but the presence of air (fire, water, air), he adds the one remaining element, earth—earth as it connotes dirt and fertility. While the narrator, the fictionalizer, can agree that the house, unlike Mrs. Mean who burns on the lawn, is cool, he dares not see the cool as something desirable. He draws instead upon a distasteful event from his childhood to remove the coolness of the Mean house from any entangling attractiveness in his mind: digging under the porch of the family house, the narrator had accidentally touched a cold, clammy water pipe covered with white slugs (104). Thus, he lumps together in this memory his fear of his father's anger (brought on by his yelling under the porch), the pale, fat Mr. Mean (in reality a sexual rival for the love of his made-up Mrs. Mean with her great, bell-like breasts—a real-life struggle of desire that the narrator tries to dissolve by making her husband into a disgusting fictional, and thereby controllable, character), and his avowed dislike of the smell of wet dirt (104).

The narrator's inclination to defy the masculine rival, both his father (whose anger is associated with the slugs) and Mrs. Mean's slug of a husband, and to manipulate Mrs. Mean, the object of his reluctant eroticism, drives him to probe beneath mere surface appearances (like those perceived by his wife, who lacks imagination [104]). He envisions himself as a surgeon cutting into a malignant growth (104). This evil core, as he sees it, is the threat that Mrs. Mean represents to masculinity. She is, in the fiction concocted by the narrator, the fertile seductress who inflicts great pain—a pain, nevertheless, that is irresistible. The children whom she beats relentlessly with her stick return again and again for more punishment, for they apparently crave her violent attentions. The fuming and fabulating voyeur is drawn irresistibly to watch her; he cannot stop (87).

Symbolically, she *is* the earth of her space, her yard. She waters her yard, making her earth moist for the growing of peonies. She kills any nascent phallus in the form of a dandelion stem that might invade and fertilize her ground (97). As in "The Pedersen Kid," again the dandelion, the upright stalk with snowy hair, the sprayer of seeds, stands for the masculine, the father. And behind the symbol, behind the fictiveness of her being, there is the specter of real life, the possibility that Mrs. Mean is not a character in a story, that she is really just a woman in the neighborhood, that she has no relationship with any narrator, that she is human and defiant of any attempt to make of her an object of art, an absolute, the opposite end of a syzygy.

The core story about the woman across the way intimates a core of reality: in watching her critically, the narrator forgets her "geologic depth, the vein of meanness deep within her earth." He has forgotten to balance her "mechanical flutter" against the "glacial movement of reality" (108). Mrs. Mean, presented amid constant reference to the four traditional elements of being—heat, moisture, air, and earth—is like being itself. Being cannot be beautiful or ugly, hot or cold, good or evil; it only *is,* and in its enormity, can swallow up the one who perceives it. The narrator appreciates this facet of reality and art when he tries unsuccessfully to fictionalize Mr. Wallace and stereotype the Mean kids.

No sooner does the narrator effect the fictional metamorphosis of the Means into fly-covered bears in a zoo than Mr. Wallace, heretofore just a name "at large" to which he attaches the words "gigantic" and "swallowing life" (108), emerges with the potential to become a character. Of course, becoming a character in this story means theriomorphosis: he is reduced, along with the Mean menagerie (bears, slugs, cows), to one of the "steers" in the new Mean-Wallace alliance (108). The neighborhood reality of ordinary, gregarious people getting together for social purposes overreaches any fiction that can be made of such interaction. And Wallace, like Mrs. Mean and Omensetter, seems truly a part of this reality, unapproachable and intractable from the standpoint of the fictionmaker. Wallace lacks respect for the narrator's word charms, preferring instead his own "omens" and "symbolings" (108–9). Wallace is, in addition, a syzygy of Mrs. Mean; like her, he is loquacious and loud and hobbles on a stick, a stick used as a weapon. If he cannot manipulate the Mean lady with his fiction skills, the fabricator finds in Wallace a good second, if not equally challenging, shot.

The narrator decides to use Wallace's interest in prophecy as the guiding metaphor, bait in which to sink the hook of his words; to match the bait and the hook, he elevates Wallace from fish to the whale of Jonah, reflecting his pronouncements about prophecy. He likewise magnifies his own role as fisherman to that of a kind of Ahab after the whale, featuring himself as bait with a harpoon in his hand in lieu of the original hook. He projects a more direct attack this time, letting himself be swallowed, carrying the harpoon down into the belly of the whale. From the moist oily stomach of the whale, he will, like Jonah, be vomited out on the dry land of a "mystery world" (109). He will achieve a verbal manipulation of his would-be character, an artistic triumph, a philosophical "wedding of opposites," the union of wet and dry that the "ancient Greek philosophers" considered to be the nature of being (109). Wallace goes for the bait, making the comment about the itching mole, the step that the narrator hopes he will take.

The narrow crack of Wallace's curiosity is widened into a cavern as the narrator, like Jethro Furber, pushes words around with consummate skill; he has found an oblique path to the earthy fire of Mrs. Mean, to whom he cannot speak, through the water-oil fishiness of Wallace, whose soul can be moved by the air of symbolic interconnections. The earth's atmosphere is like the skin around the body. There is continual interplay between various sets of elements, between skin blemishes and lust, for example. The narrator's imagination takes flight as he weaves the web of associations for his seemingly gullible listener.

The words engendered by the "soaring" of the narrator's fancy indeed have their effect; Wallace, called a "monster," and compared to Jonah's whale and Goliath, falls under the sway of rhetoric. The compelling structure of the narrator's words (like the deadly power of the "stone symbolic" [109], the smooth pebble that flew from the sling of the poet-king, killing Goliath, putting out the light of his eyes [109], and like the "joy of stone" equated with dead roach carcasses in "Order of Insects," [170]), an absolute order found in the absolute antithesis of easy life, makes old Wallace reveal the location of the moles on his wife's body. Like a Satan or a Jethro Furber, this wordtwister moves the old man's childlike line of vision from the celestial to the infernal. Wallace seems to be genuinely frightened about the omens inherent in moles (111).

The old man veers momentarily away from faith and love and confidence in some transcendent equilibrium into the heresy of gnostic desire for knowledge. The narrator is sure that there are moles on the body of Mrs. Wallace and that Mr. Wallace would burn in the consuming desire to *know,* to know the frightening, but wonderful correlation between the structure of the heavens and the map of moles on the skin. Like Adam and Eve and all of us, Wallace wants to approach the delicious thin edge of knowing and believing, of perceiving and being.

Wallace, even though he does reveal to the narrator the locations of his wife's blemishes, keeps his own blemishes a secret. In the wake of the narrator's attempt to control him, to make of him another fictional puppet, to disillusion him by asserting the opposite of his original proposition ("all omens are imaginings" [115]), he bolts, uncrushed, and goes elsewhere (to the Means) for his conversation.

The Means, like the Omensetters, do not make the proper intellectual connections, do not wall themselves away in thought and word: rather, they love and act and laugh loudly, they congregate and share. While perceiving relationships between the self and the world and verbally projecting those connections into knowledge can lead to a glimpse of beauty, going too far with the process can lead to deep unhappiness; beauty in its static artificiality is monstrous, inhuman, cold, evil. Absolutely formal good, and absolutely formal evil, are indistinguishable. As in butterfly collecting, to redeem the formal elegance of design from the desecration of time is to kill the specimen. Beauty projected into timeless artifact is a kind of wickedness that "rests rather on the pale brow of every saviour who to save us all from death first kills" (113). Casting human beings by the artifice of fiction into characters is wicked, unnatural. Wallace seeks instead the "sweet times" that lie out of range of verbal artillery, beyond fictional order, beyond deathly abstraction. So, too, eventually, does the narrator: the fictional "conjuror" tries to penetrate by stealth the "house of love" (116), the Means' house, where the Wallaces and Mrs. Cramm have gathered.

The interloper gets only as far as the garage when he suddenly realizes that he, as narrator, cannot enter the reality of the house and the people that he has watched from his fortress, and that, in his state, "sweet times" for him do not exist: he cannot enter fully into love so long as he clings to his artistic voyeurism. He knows that for him the Means can never be "the world"; he knows that he has "gone too far" (117). The narrator becomes suddenly aware that he is a prisoner of his godlike way of perceiving and dealing with the world; he can only *desire* to enter the Means' house. Although he thinks that it will be only a matter of days until he can slip inside the Means' house through the back screen, he will always be frustrated as long as he attempts to enter unseen. He will never find a rear entrance; disguised as the unseen narrator, he will never reach closure with the house and the love in that house. He cannot, however, remain encased in his sheath of fictions; reality continues to rear its monstrous head. Not even his fictional notions, those within the carefully concocted fabrications of his mind, are exempt from the creeping incursions of an inherently extraliterary world. Made to fit the narrator's inner world of absolutes, Ames, the eldest Mean boy, a victim, a character that the storyteller has attempted to make "good," heroic, a fairytale character abused by a wicked mother, persists, nevertheless, in being "nasty, unnaturally nasty" (103). Not even characters in a story can remain untouched by the taint of the world, by deep associations with worldly objects that will not go away regardless of the intensity of verbal conjuring.

"Icicles"

The hulking specter of the world that looms behind any realm of language is the theme of "Icicles," a variation on the larger thematic umbrella of Gass's work based on the writer's preoccupation with fiction and reality. Although hesitant myself to summarize anything in Wittgenstein, I admire such attempts by others. Clyde Hardin states succinctly the essence of the arguments in *Philosophical Investigations* that deal with phenomenal language: "Language is a social function which depends upon the possibility of correction by another person; without this social context there is no distinction between following a rule and thinking that one is following a rule, so that a private language becomes a meaningless babble. There is no objective check upon memory mistakes in a purely phenomenal language, so that one can never know whether today's rules are the same as those of yesterday."[5] The social obligations of language make the fabrication of idealized fictional worlds as totally distinct from the real world an impossible although understandable and even admirable task. Gass reiterates in this piece, as elsewhere, his affirmation, but ultimate rejection, of pristine verbal artifice; working within this tensional state between fiction and real life, Gass again manifests those elastic bands that bind him to the realist tradition, a tradition against which he contends and which he attempts to modify.

Escape into the world of the ideal is the desire and impossible goal of most Gass characters. Fender, as a familiar element in the ongoing allegory of expression and being, reflects both the situational and the temporal nature of language mentioned in Hardin's summary of Wittgenstein above. Fender, the name and focus of fictional discourse, functions in the story as a "fender"-off of incoming sensation, invading pulses from outside the self that weaken the process of conceptual assimilation of reality, and a "freezerless" would-be freezer of ever-flowing time and linguistic certainty.

Gass, true to expectations, builds this story around a few key words, words that, like Fender's icicles, acquire layers of substance as the story develops. The first of these is the word *icicle* itself. The word is matched to a phenomenon of time, the formation of an object of great static elegance out of fluidity, a flux itself in turn born in the melting of those formally intricate crystals, snow flakes. Fender describes a heavy snowfall at night followed by the sun's melting of the snow on the roof and the subsequent formation of the runny slush and then the elongation of the slush into glasslike icicles (120). Time, the movement of the earth around the sun, engenders a moment that seems halted, immune from its own ravages, immobilized and lifeless in the form of the icicle. There is a "first," and then a "later." Like everything, night and day, ignorance and knowledge, innocence and experience, icicles come into being and change constantly, are opaque and then crystalline, are and then are not. Also like all things, they are dual, they are products of the interplay of opposites, they move along lines of syzygy. If they are brilliant and extremely beautiful, they also are ugly and hide things as they are. If icicles form sheets of dazzling curtains that reflect the light of streetlamps, they also hide the qualities of the house as viewed from the street, making, in terms of the real estate business, a difficult showing and therefore a difficult sale. Icicles, in other words, can have a negative commercial impact (120–21).

Fender, eating his meat pie, looks out the window at the winter grayness and makes the immediate association between the barren iciness and his cold loneliness. He further amalgamates this ice with his pie to form another model of time. The hot pie burns his mouth; he thinks of putting his scorched tongue to the cold windowpane to experience the healing of opposites. He stops, however, when he thinks that his boss Pearson (Piercing) might see him do a strange thing and think the worst about such strange behavior in an adult, a businessman. This piercing of his private ritual would not be good for his career. Thoughts of career lead to thoughts of business in general and the cycles of business. These cycles tie in again with his pie and the ice and Pearson. As the light "pierces" the pie, Fender, disturbed by the icicles outside, thinks about the way companies lower prices during periods of waning sales to spark consumer buying. He equates the good sense of buying great quantities of meat pies during these bargain times and placing them in a freezer with business savvy. This prudence, based on the cycle of business activity, is the kind of prudence he is obliged by his profession, and urged by Pearson, to exert. His failure to own a freezer thus emphasizes his failure in the real estate business—failure to look ahead to the opening of new supermarkets or banks or office complexes and to capitalize on their impact on the value of surrounding property. Freezing pies when they are on sale is like freezing a moment in the business cycle; such capture of the moment in business time is as desirable as catching the beautiful moment in art.

Ice and time suggest another extension of the rigidity–fluidity continuum: other people, the outside world, the reality of business. Sitting in his house behind the ice makes Fender think of the two types of people with whom he is obliged to get along but with whom he is utterly uncomfortable and unsuccessful. The first is the prospect, the customer. The word *prospects,* in Fender's mind, is inhabited by conflicting connotations; the sign has two registers of symbolism. It is slippery; it is suggestive of pickles; it is supposed to mean, for a real estate salesman like Fender, a vehicle for success, an opportunity to make money, to think in terms of gold, a chance for independence and freewheeling, fresh air and expansion. But prospects for Fender mean further isolation and failure. The connotation of gold is present in the word, but so are beards, dirt, stony biscuits, tin utensils, the smell of mules, bad water, and mirage (121). Pickles are green counterparts to icicles, vegetable protrusions that connote spring and youth, the phallus; they stand in taut syzygy to icicles as "needles" to "fingers" (135), swords to pens (Pearson is pictured as having fallen on the sharp tip of an icicle in the manner of a Roman falling on his sword). Glick holds a pen, a green pen that reminds Fender of a pickle, between his teeth in the way cinema pirates hold knives in their mouths.

The "pickly" component of the word "prospects" also extends axial cords to the other characters in this story and others in the collection, drawing them in to the core of the controlling system of images. The first that Fender thinks of is Glick, the "wiseman," the "joker—green all winter like a pine" (122). Glick, whose name is a composite of phonetic intensives (*gl* suggests liquid, slippery brightness; *ick* connotes smallness and sudden cessation[6]), is a mixture of several images: he is the green-coated killer in "The Pedersen Kid," the promise of springtime liberation in the depth of winter's bondage; and he makes us think of the dandelions, vegetable phalluses in "Mrs. Mean." He knows how to talk in a winning way to Isabelle and thus is a kind of rival to Fender for the attentions of Isabelle, a dream woman whom Fender can only equate with the cold, formal beauty of the icicles. Even though in Fender's mind Glick is the "kid" in the real estate office whom Fender is supposed to take under his wing, Glick offers advice to Fender and appears to have control of his work, reversing the old–young (teacher–student) polarity between the two (122). Glick, with a fawning manner and a fishlike face, is a thoroughly knowledgeable collector of flowers (which he dries and presses). Fender, failing to make the connection between Glick's attempt to preserve the beauty of spring in his dried flowers and his own worship of the brilliance of winter imprisoned momentarily in icicles, chides the younger man for such egregious foolishness (141). Glick's dead-flowery, pickly foolishness extends also into his great facility for speech; he creates from words, the dead Latin words for his dead flowers and the trite, dead words from real estate advertising, a bounding commentary on the events of the office that always draws Isabelle, to Fender's chagrin, into a "duet" of heightened verbiage, mutually flirtatious and derisive of the older rival.

Glick transforms the language of real estate advertising into what for Fender is the dreaded "recital," an ironic verbal emancipation (matching the actual freedom brought on by the collapse of the firm) from the bondage that Pearsons' office has exerted over all of them: "sordid work room . . . Yes indeedy, says Isabelle. . . . a ratty-off-hole. . . . Don't we know it, says Isabelle . . . a god-damned grave . . . holder in fee simple of Leo Glick and Charlie Fender . . . And also me-oh, says Isabelle" (146–47).

At home, holed-up inside his ice-encrusted house, out of a job, eating his pot pie (that has become symbolic of the business cycle), Fender remembers Glick's jangling word-spew. He tries to oppose to the landslide of images tumbling out of Glick's sour, pickle-stained mouth his own symbols of inner "real" estate and business drawn from the hot, liquid image-inducing world of his pie. Fender's incantation consists of the enumeration of building features like elevators and dumbwaiters and the counting of peas in his pie. He reiterates to himself that he is not green, not green like the infamous Glick (147).

Green Glick, fish-faced preserver of flowers, word-bender and pickly phallic suitor of Isabelle, is the symbol of spring and liberation from the icy rigidity of winter. He is a composite of the green-coated killer, Omensetter and Pike (as fish-gods and progenitor-saviors), and Furber the phrase-bender (who demonstrates by his words the inefficacy of ingratiation with the world as well as the germ of his redemption). Glick, who speaks in names of flowers and imagines the icicle, not as an object of beauty, but rather as an instrument of death for his boss, is a polarization of the elements inside Fender, what Fender might be if he were young and not trapped in icy sterility, in lifeless nonbeing, himself an icicle. Glick is successful at dealing with property, acquiring property (including Isabelle's ear) without himself becoming anybody's property. But Fender is only overwhelmed, not redeemed, by his knowledge of and dialogue with Glick; even the wooden arms of Fender's chair possess him, turn him to wood. And, finally, the property that is Fender, a human place, a person become his house, is for sale: "you're For Sale, Fender . . . I hope you see humor in it" (158). But his words cannot give him the distance and the power of humor. He gives up on verbal escape altogether, decides on silence, and, crushed by the outside world of youth and life (symbolized by his imagined avalanche of boys in the snow), falls into babble: "Selling's not all fuck luck, nossir. Not all fuck luck . . . fuckaluck" (160).

Immobilized in time like an icicle or a frozen pie, he has reached a deathly beauty, the beauty of the ice.

"Order of Insects"

The metamorphosis of a human being into a house, his own house, can mean personification of lifelessness and can be evidence of spiritual exhaustion, of being beaten into numbness by an outside world. But, as in "The Order of Insects," the everyday world, chaotic and oppressive, can be brought into focus and sacralized by means of contact with its "other," in this case the carcasses of dead roaches.

The narrator of this piece is a housewife who has just moved into a house; but even though the house is new to her, otherwise her life remains unchanged. Her routine of wifely chores determines her being. She says again and again that she is the wife of the house, that she keeps it clean and smoothly running, and that she lives amid blocks, surrounded by the voices of children, and in constant interruption. Her repetition of these facts becomes a refrain that punctuates the story. In the midst of this hectic existence, the woman stops to consider the archenemy of the clean, feminine, motherly life: roaches. The ugly bugs are always being discovered dead; the cat paws them; the wife, looking the other way, sucks them up, listening with excitement and terror as they dance up the pipe of her vacuum cleaner (165). The narrator's former dwelling had been infested with live roaches, fast, fuzzy, almost electric with life; but such bugs, full of vital motion, as her existence had been full of domestic business and unending activity, had never made her stop and look and ponder the way the lifeless ones now do. Like Furber to Omensetter, the invisible voyeur-narrator to Mrs. Mean, the wife is drawn ineluctably to her polar opposite; typical of Gass's oppositionally developed, dialectically reversed characters, she enters into the familiar lines of dialectical tension; she begins the study of the silent carapaces, "no study for a woman . . . bugs" (164). Like Tiresias, at the sight of vipers wrapped in mating coils, death surprised in the act of bringing life, the wife turns, as if entranced, to things of the diametrically other kind. The deathly order, like Fender's icicles, commands her attention and draws her out of her role as a woman afraid of roaches.

Recalling a Dante who has stopped in the middle of the highway of life to look into the eternity of death, the woman, moved by the seemingly immortal structure of the corpses, rehearses her ordinary fears and contrasts them to the most authentic and terrible fear of all—death: "So it was amid the worries of our ordinary life I bent, innocent and improperly armed, over the bug that had come undone" (168–69).

The wife's former belief that love is not really a matter of structure and life inextricably welded to turbulence yields momentarily to the opposite view. She appreciates the vibrant excitement in exquisite composition and exults in the pleasures "of stone" (170). Her taking up of the study of bugs, her acquisition thereby of a tainted outlook (170), her display of intense interest in a masculine kind of pursuit, her addiction to the hobby that dreadfully modifies her vision: all frighten her children. They cannot understand that "either-or" (man or woman, mother or father, life or death, love or artifice) can in a moment be transubstantiated into "both-and." The woman, because of her imagination (which she no longer owns), experiences, like Furber and the other self-incarcerated narrators typical in Gass's fiction, "the joy of stone." But because of her love, she knows that this "point of view of a god" (171) does not square with her role as a housewife: "were I not a continuing woman, I could disarm my life, find peace and order everywhere; . . . I could leave and let my bones play cards and spank the children . . . Peace. How can I think of such ludicrous things—beauty and peace, the dark soul of the world—for I am the wife of the house, concerned for the rug, tidy and punctual, surrounded by blocks" (171).

The wife thus avoids the snare of absolute beauty, resists being mesmerized into an unhealthy avoidance of life by a simple, seductive, but sterile aestheticism. Like Dante, she resurfaces to life after having gazed at "the dark soul of the world." Like Gass's ideal reader, she has read the "geometric precision" and the "splendid corruption" in the roach carcasses, and has allowed her imagination to soar almost out of sight; but in the end, she has realized that beauty is just an ordinary fat cockroach after all, the kind that frightens ordinary housewives (171). As a result of her fatal brush with beauty, she has returned to love and to a fuller life; she has gained a both-and dimension.

"In the Heart of the Heart of the Country"

The concept of both/and as opposed to either/or anchors the theme of "In the Heart of the Heart of the Country," the title work and most popular story in this collection. Tom LeClair, in his study of Don DeLillo's novels, has called the kind of writing that so-called postmodern experimenters like Gaddis, Pynchon, and Coover do "systems" fiction. Based on the "new biology" of von Bertalanffy, the systems sociology of Talcott Parsons, and the holistic psychology of Anatole Rappoport, this view of fiction opposes conventional mechanistic, commonsense perceptions and analyses of the world. One of the central ideas of LeClair's category is that "the either/or logic of mechanism is inadequate for the both/and relations—the simultaneity—of living systems." Living systems are open and circular and therefore not amenable to "mechanistic principles used to analyze closed systems of entities in linear chains of cause and effect." Open, circular systems are "dynamic processes that combine energy and information in reciprocal relations"; they are "self-organizing and self-correcting," and tend toward equilibrium or homeostasis."[7] "In the Heart of the Heart of the Country" is a kind of systems fiction.

Since little "happens" in this narrative system, what we may loosely refer to as a story line is easy to summarize. A poet, having traveled far and wide, comes to a small Indiana town called B . . . , settles into a house, and lives the life of "retirement from love" (173). In thirty-six fairly short bursts of prose bearing titles like WEATHER, VITAL DATA, and MY HOUSE, brilliant blurbs that orbit the thematic center of the work, the nameless narrator describes the town in which he has chosen to live. Because of its graphic detail and "stark surface," writes Arthur Saltzman, some critics have found in this story a "singular example of literary documentary which would appear to betray the author's debt to the literary realist program."[8] But, as we have seen, Gass avoids this standard interpretation: he maintains that the town is in no way to be taken as a real place.[9]

Being "truthful" about the town is the central problem. The beginning of the story echoes Yeats's "Sailing to Byzantium" ("And therefore I have sailed the seas and come / to the holy city of Byzantium"[10]): "So I have sailed the seas and come . . . to B . . . / a small town fastened to a field in Indiana" (172). Like Yeats's Byzantium, a place of the mind, art, mythic wisdom—a sanctuary of "unageing intellect" separate from the corporal, this "B . . ." is also a holy city, a sacred ground that grows out of the surrounding vacant expanse of fields. These fields, this surrounding land, however, by analogy with Yeats's "dying animal," are dying. Frederick Busch, in his incisive essay on this story, considers Gass's Indiana town coterminous with Yeats's "heart . . . sick with desire" (line 21) as well as with his Byzantium in that both "heart" and "town" are attached to something, the heart to a "dying animal" and the town to fields: "The field, then, the land, the earth, is analogous to a dying animal. Gass's narrator may be trapped in what he has wished to flee: time, which makes the animals—and poets—die."[11]

This is the source of the persona of Jethro Furber, "Fur-burr" (*OL,* 41), a burr stuck in the fur of an animal, the desire for the timeless formality of beauty that haunts all human beings, reminding them always of the horror of their mortality and of the impossibility of finding a refuge in artifice. This is the same burr that Hans talks about in "The Pedersen Kid." A reality exists behind the dreams, lies, and fabrications that hits the perceiver of that reality with such force that he ends up "raving" (17); those ravings are the beginnings of story, a story that Hans proceeds to make up about how the killer, like the Pedersen kid, came out of the storm (17–18); a story that sounds plausible to Jorge but that does not square with reality (18). The truth, then, of any narrative lies in the sounding as opposed to the being, concatenations of words that form verbal artifice in syzygy with the seeking heart attached to a lump of living matter doomed by time. Meaning in literature, thus, is not a matter of choosing either pure artifice or dying animal, but rather a matter of recognizing that meaning is *both* "such a form as Grecian goldsmiths make" (line 27, "Sailing to Byzantium") *and* a mortal heart sick with the desire for eternity.

Yeats's dying animal, therefore, has been transformed into a vegetal symbol of time, a field, a space for the cyclic reappearance and obliteration of vegetation, an open, season-governed expanse that has become a prison of time (the time that kills animals, vegetables, and people) for the town, a "holy city," a timeless refuge. In this parody of the pastoral, of the finding of ideal love in the country, Gass sets forth allegorically his basic theory of fiction: the world must be reduced to sequential sounds, words, like musical notes; these words are then to be reconstituted to make a self, a place that both is and is not of the world. The reciprocal (to make use of a term from systems theory) relationship between artifice and life is at the core of this story; as Busch rightly states, the narrator "is the town, the town is he."[12]

The narrator does indeed present a detailed description of a small town in the Midwest. He can look out his window and see what anyone in his position would see. The town's neatness and shadiness is stereotypically attractive; a plastic deer even graces one lawn. The railroad tracks hum when the train approaches, the forsythia sings. The people include familiar kinds of characters, with names like Billy Holzclaw, Westbrook, Horsefall, Mott, and curious personalities like Janet Jakes the irascible teacher and old Mrs. Desmond, symbolic of death. Rhythmic, evocative description gives the story a standard literary "life." The reader can almost inhale the heavy atmosphere of midwestern tedium, of cigarette-smoking housewives at the washermat, old men tottering in the street, and the dank smell of livestock in the town.

Such passages suggest a hard-driving verisimilitude; most readers, especially those who see only the surface of the story, find among these images a realistic accuracy that both is, and is not, at the heart of the heart of this country of "B. . . ." As William Gass states concerning Malcolm Lowry's *Under the Volcano,* a thematic counterpart to this work, "Lowry is constructing a place, not describing one" (*FFL,* 57). The narrator takes in these details, bits and fragments of a reality, of life in an Indiana town, and, like a musical composer with his notes, remakes the town in marks that can be restored to being every time a reader reads them. Of course, these notes do not merely describe, do not merely render a reality. These details do not ape reality, as history tries to do, but rather they constitute a verbal complex that itself is a world.

The narrator's world is an imaginary construct; the reader enters not only a town like other towns across the heartland of America, but he enters as well the mind and body of the fictional focus that we call the narrator. The narrator is both an instrument of perception and that perception itself. He reorganizes his "B . . ." according to his own lights; in this reconstitution, he reveals the way in which he views the world. As Busch says, "Because he has created it—because he may *be* it—if we know the way he sees his world, we may know him."[13] Readers are both like the narrator and very much unlike him. Their thought processes are rarely linear as is the usual story structure. Flesh-and-blood human beings draw in the data of daily life haphazardly, "irregularly," and "at widely separated times," and then arrange these items idiosyncratically. They are not accustomed, however, to encounter such manipulation in literature. This irregularity in the narrator's poetic way of "diddling" with the reality of the town to make up a fictional self out of its "menacing phrases" is puzzling to readers who expect the conventional linear ordering and referential quality of fiction.

Neither do readers expect a narrator to mesh with the reality that he seeks to render in language. The blocks of text labeled THE CHURCH seem to have little in common with and little connection to normal literary perspective. One section bearing this title is about a basketball game, another contains a vision of the church's steeple as a witch's hat; yet another section identifies his house as a sacred edifice, a building with mysterious, blue-gray windows and a holy interior to match (179). Finally, he makes of himself a holy precinct like the church: "I think I shall hat my head with a steeple; turn church; devour people" (184). This last rhythmic representation of self as church echoes the children's rhyme (a device used extensively in *Omensetter's Luck*) that accompanies an interlocking of fingers to form a church with the hands: "Here is the church and here is the steeple / Open the door and here are the people." The narrator here captures the childlike incantation and accompanying hand movements that create a church from fingers and thumbs: by putting on the witch's hat–steeple, he himself becomes a sacred artifact as does his house. The children's verse, reducing data from the outside world to stylized language and creating thereby a realm of sacred space, becomes a way of organizing the narrator's self. This fusion of self, house, and church is driven by what Mircea Eliade calls man's "ontological thirst . . . religious man's will to take his stand at the very heart of the real, at the Center of the World," the symbolism of which is "the formative principle not only of countries, cities, temples, and palaces but also of the humblest human dwelling, be it the tent of a nomad hunter, the shepherd's yurt, or the house of the sedentary cultivator."[14]

As the body has eyes to let in and transform stimuli from the outside world, so the sacred house has bewitching windows that hold reality under their spell. Like Ortega's window, the glass that separates the narrator from his world is the artistic medium; the poet can see real things, but only "in the glass": leaves do not move except in the glass (195). The artificial world of the poet's perception, like the carapaces of the dead roaches in "Order of Insects," is dead. The poet's window is his grave; what fills its frame is dead (195). The windows reflect the narrator because his world is, like Yeats's Byzantium, a refuge of pure artifice. The world and the poet meet, and swim together, in the glass (196–97). His artistic elaboration changes the process of perception: instead of the things outside merely finding expression, the expression dominates the things outside, making of them a world of the mind. Like most of Gass's narrators, this one has fallen into the trap of his own words.

In converting the town and the country to fiction, in "turning church," the narrator manages to "devour people" (184)—that is, he transubstantiates them into literary characters. Although these fictional creatures smack of the real world, they are merely symbols, pieces of tile in the intricate mosaic of the narrator's self. The "golden tomgirl," the supposed source of the love from which the narrator is in mock-pastoral retirement, is portrayed in realistic detail; her description is as explicit as those of the contemporary pulp novels on the rack at the drugstore: she has the slouching gait of a teenager and blushes with her whole body under the wanton gaze of her lover. In a manner used by few lovers in pastorals, the poet of the story speaks to his beloved: "You used to waddle when you walked because my sperm between your legs was draining into a towel" (175). But, despite this graphic, almost tactile image of sexual intimacy, the girl, like everything else in B . . . (Byzantium?), is only a creature of words, a figure out of Mark Twain (179). Her bosom can be inflated with a kiss, her skin dispersed by gentleness, her womb entered from within (196). This woman is only a poem; the poem, even though it appears to do so, does not reflect a living lover, but is itself both artifact and lover—she (it) represents the totalizing possibility of language: the sperm dripping from between her legs is really only an "endless worm of words" (201). The woman, like the poem, lives only in the cold pane of the glass. Loving the beautiful structure of the mind is deathly: the narrator, in loving her, has fallen to his death (201). The woman, as poem—verbal precinct, thus is a pit constructed by the poet; and like Milton's Satan, who fell in love with his own autonomous world of verbal fabrication, she falls doomed into that very world.

Other "devoured" people are portrayed with apparent verisimilitude, only later to reveal deceptively made-up natures. They turn out to be merely additional vessels to contain the narrator's fictive syrup; other roads along which the poet can extend himself into the world. The first of these is Billy Holzclaw, a counterpart, a foil of sorts to the narrator. As with the poet, Billy and his house are one, and both components of Holzclaw are in a trap—not spatial or verbal, but temporal. Time is in the process of robbing Billy of his being. Time destroys his body and his house simultaneously (200–1). He is the polar opposite of the narrator: his windows are boarded up—he has no panes to swim in (202); he collects things—but not images and concepts; he appears to have nothing inside (the poet wonders what there is inside Billy) whereas the poet himself has everything inside; and he knows by touching and smelling, not thinking and writing. Finally, Billy has nothing important to say, nor, ironically, any control of his torrent of wild words; but he tries, nevertheless, to make some verbal contact with his opposite, the poet. He talks breathlessly about the weather (179). "Weather" may be a euphemism for no-content in Billy's speech, but weather is his ontological emblem: he is the personification of time and its cyclic path to destruction. Like Furber walking in ritual magic around and around on his stones, Billy must strive to keep the weeds of summer from choking access to his house (190). These same weeds in winter bear the threat of death. But the destruction of Billy Holzclaw, who merely survives in his poor environment without the benefits of imagination and language, would be undesirable to the poet for selfish reasons. He prefers that Billy remain as he is—he finds some negative reassurance in his presence. Billy exerts some mysterious oppositional pull against the narrator (190). What Billy means to the poet is what animals in a zoo mean to a city dweller, what Omensetter means to Furber, what Jorge means to the Pedersen kid, what summer means to winter: being comes from the tugging of diametrically opposed forces.

There is a kind of violence, a throbbing anger, in these strained dialectical juxtapositions of metaphor. The rage to touch the world, and the frustrating impossibility to do so artistically, can only enrage the poet. He must recognize that children, young girls let out of school, can indeed enjoy comradeship and innocent affection in the flesh-and-blood version of an Indiana town, an alternative place in the real world that opposes his sacred extension of himself, his "B . . . ," and at the same time reaches precise congruency with it. Young girls can be real beings as well as "tomgirls," happy, careless children as well as fictional props (skiffs on a river in a Mark Twain novel), or the fictional abstraction of fiction itself personified as an aged, loquacious woman, at once child, mother, and widow, who, like a story, keeps on stringing words together to avoid the inevitable end, emblemizing the transitoriness of life (184).

The brevity of life and the inevitability of death are most vividly presented, however, in the polarity of two elements within the realm of "B . . ." and two completely outside its boundaries. The first of these dialectical splits is between the poet and his cat, Mr. Tick. The poet-narrator, because he has made up his world and because that world has him in thrall, finds in his cat a being that pulls at his own intensely conscious human selfhood from across a taut diameter, a line that extends to a point outside the time and the space of "B . . .": the cat is not really in (in the narrator's sense of "living in") the poet's house (a virtual or word-projected refuge constructed outside of, but nevertheless containing his own body), but lives truly "in" its cat-body, "his long tail rhyming with his paws" (183); the total cat is "let out" of the house (of fiction) and into the shrubbery, but only the eyes of the narrator can pass through the glass of the windows and out into seasonal seeds and leaves (183). The cat's being is coterminous with its body; therefore, the cat, like Omensetter, stands for the purely somatic nature of life, the impossible dream of reentry to Eden.

Mr. Tick, as his name also indicates, is outside the time (as well as the space) restrictions of storylands like "B. . . ." Tick is the initial element of time reduced to machinery—the working of a clock. By naming this movement "tick" and its successor "tock," we fictionalize the clock's mechanical sound; and, as Frank Kermode writes, "by this fiction we humanize it, make it talk our language."[15] The duration of this artificially marked interval is temporal form, a model for plot. Eliade would call this staking out of ordered interval from disorganized time the ritual reconstitution of the "first appearance of . . . reality."[16] Kermode agrees: "Of course, it is we who provide the fictional difference between the two sounds; tick is our word for a physical beginning, tock our word for an end. We say they differ. What enables them to be different is a special kind of middle. We can perceive duration only when it is organized."[17] Mr. Tick, "coiled like a fetus" (184), is just that: the beginning of life that implies an end, that holds out the hope of somehow creeping back into the past, recreating childhood, being totally in consonance with the body, living innocently and thoughtlessly. Mr. Tick personifies the opening of the fictive interval that we call life and at the same time he closes off any escape from that end. Like the voyeur-narrator in "Mrs. Mean," the poet, thinking about the children in the schoolhouse, feels the overpowering impulse to cease making up his world and yield himself to real life (187). Forsaking momentarily his "sophistries about spirit, mind, and breath" (202), he decides that the cat's life is better: "Body equals being, and if your weight goes down, you are the less" (202).

The narrator, in his reverie about his childhood, cannot shake off the presence of rot and flies: that caked flypaper, for instance, in his grandmother's house where pleasant kitchen smells mingled with odors of farm animals. He knew the house in an "unchaste" way, the way flies know life (203–4). This amalgam of "un-chastity," decay, dream-lover, and childhood nostalgia is, like Yeats's gyre, an extreme that contains within it seeds of its opposite. The romantic notion of childhood oneness with nature is not exactly true. Like the idealized pastoral theme, the georgic conception of life on the farm, "childhood is a lie of poetry" (205). Honesty and "unchastity" go together as do poetic dishonesty and aseptic, chaste sterility. Like the burr in the fur mentioned in other Gass stories, decay and corruption stand behind real childhood just as they underlie all of life.

The mythic ideal of the tick without the tock, of Mr. Tick's careless unity of self and body, is alien to human existence and therefore is also a lie of poetry. Flies, flying maggots that feed on rotting life, are paradoxically the most lively of creatures. And flies, in their harsh syzygy with carefree childhood and life-perpetuating fruit, delineate life with brutal clarity. The narrator tells of his work in the orchards where rotten fruit and swarms of flies on his body were the expected state of things. These loathsome pests, feeding on death, are the antithesis of death: they are nature's corrective for corruption; they, like old Mrs. Desmond, live by a total preoccupation with death. Like

Holzclaw, the flies are "windowless," having no art and no self-appreciation, only the humming drive toward survival, the harmony of sugar. This unabashed surrender to natural law, that everything must have an opposing force, that what goes in one direction must be pulled back in the other, is the genesis of what I have referred to as syzygy in narrative technique. Gass's composition by syzygy is allegorized in the symbolic linking of church and gymnasium, religion and basketball.

There is in the town of "B . . ." a church with a witch's-hat steeple and a poet who metaphorically puts on that steeple-hat and "turns church," as we have seen. Poetic artifice and theology are thus presented as one and the same: both are fictional mediations of unapproachable reality. There is another section titled THE CHURCH, however, that is confusing in that it has apparently little to do with religion. It is a vivid sketch of a basketball game.

Gass's skill in metaphorical probing reaches its height in this section. This church service has no pious words, no boring sermons, no canonical liturgies, no exhausted platitudes. There is only the wild shouting of a community drawn together by love—the honest love of the game. This blissfully oblivious communication is analogous to the pulsating hum of flies united by their zest for sugar. Calling to mind the wordless initiations of ancient mystery cults,[18] the worshippers in this religion merely watch the prancing and whirling of pubescent cheerleaders whose short skirts reveal their bloomered buttocks, young men leaping and running through pools of light, the bounding ball as it moves to the roar of voices in the crowd (206). Sexuality, youth, and natural law coalesce in this perfect ritual of love and community. The ball, like the bouncing stones skipped across the surface of water by Omensetter, rises from the hard floor and caroms along in a continuous cycle, up and down, between the tick of the whistle beginning play and the tock of the ending buzzer. The dialectic of poet and the world finds ritual expression in this up-and-down cycle; there is the elation of "rising above" and the humility of falling again to the dead immobility of stone or roach carapace. If the poet desires to fly above the ordinary world on his wings of language, to soar above others like a balloon, to rise so high that any shit excreted would "miss nobody" (189), he must also be prepared to fall like Satan from arrogant self-love into that other world that by its force of opposition turns his window into a cemetery (195).

I agree with Frederick Busch's summary of "In the Heart of the Heart of the Country": "It is a work of majestic profundity, dazzling complexity and wit. It celebrates the imagination and condemns it; the condemnation celebrates life."[19] My opinion is that these words can apply to the entire collection, fragments of brilliant prose fiction that separate William Gass from the

deconstructive, postmodernist extreme in experimental writing as well as reiterate and underscore his quest for a revitalization of the threadbare conventions of the realist tradition. These stories fix Gass in my mind as a precursor
of what LeClair has called systems fiction, fiction that is configural, ecosys-
temic, transactional. While these stories undoubtedly place Gass in the camp
of those whom Richard Kostelanetz would classify as saboteurs of the realist
"masterpiece-mentality,"[20] they reveal a writer who, like Coover, Pynchon,
Gaddis, Barth, and DeLillo, transcends the excesses and trivialities of
postmodernism, summarized by Ronald Sukenick in his "law of mosaics"
("how to deal with parts in the absence of wholes").[21]

William Gass, in these stories, demonstrates his allegiance to what LeClair
calls "the methods of 'earlier times': metaphor, the paradigmatic over the
syntagmatic, the abstract mixed with the concrete, macro and micro
worlds."[22] This wholeness and profundity place William Gass and "In the
Heart of the Heart of the Country" (story and collection) in a kind of "uneasy
peace" with the "equal powers," with both the innovative forces of today and
the masterpieces of earlier times.

Chapter Four

Willie Masters' Lonesome Wife: "Skating on One Galosh"

The stories of *In the Heart of the Heart of the Country* are typical of William Gass's fiction in that most of his works feature dialectical cleavage between characters and sets of characters, character relationships that allegorize concepts and make up the governing configurations that in their turn constitute Gass's narrative. The central Gass persona is generally a narrator who self-consciously reflects on the fictional world that he finds himself in the act of composing. The reader is thus left in his traditional position: a location outside the dialogue, at the third point of the triangle consisting of narrator, narrative world, and reader. In *Willie Masters' Lonesome Wife,* however, the text calls out to the reader directly, inviting confrontation and interaction, setting up a colloquy between reader and text, or, as Larry McCaffery states, the engagement of the reader in a "dialogue about the book he is reading."[1] Arthur Saltzman summarizes this shift in narrative perspective: "whereas we contemplate Jethro Furber as he insulates himself with language against perilous surroundings—we are able to discriminate between both camps from our vantage point—we lose that conventional distance in *Willie Masters'.* Babs Masters' needs are blatant and insatiable; she demands our undivided attention, as a jealous lover keeps her partner on a short leash."[2]

Because of this straightforward entanglement of the reader's attention with the book itself rather than any "subject" or aspect of reality for which the book is merely a vehicle, this work is a prime example of metafiction. I agree with McCaffery that Gass's novella is a "remarkably pure and interesting example of the genre (metafictional or anti-novel)."[3] Although Gass is not fond of labels, and, as I have pointed out earlier, particularly resents being called postmodern, this is clearly one exaggerated attempt on his part to do something flagrantly antirealist and unconventional, to create, in Jerome Klinkowitz's words, an aesthetic system that "by claiming to be nothing else . . . becomes a real entity."[4] Of course, rhetorical systems cannot become completely autonomous; as phenomenologists like Merleau-Ponty lament, language, while inherently cut off from the objective world, the signified, can acquire life only by pointing back to that world of things.[5] But Gass, in this work especially, seeks to make the reader as aware as possible of the fictional product as an entity palpable and visibly concrete in itself. This preoccupation with the book as an object made of paper and ink points in a direction seemingly contrary to Gass's usual emphasis on literature as oral performance.[6] He criticizes Dreiser and even Pynchon for writing only for the page, not the ear.[7] That is, however, exactly how one is forced to read *Willie Masters' Lonesome Wife*. It is not so much that Gass abandons his usual musicality in this piece; rather, he is after an overt metafictional statement about the importance of fiction presented and appreciated as visual artifice and not reality. Gass stated in an interview that in *Willie Masters'* he was trying some new things that did not work out. He wanted to find some kind of spatial point on which to center the music of the work. The results he considers to be "amateurish" ("I was skating on one galosh"). The book's success is predicated on visual effects produced for the most part by a layout designer—not Gass's writing.[8]

Willie Masters' Lonesome Wife, to be sure, veers from the progressive modernism of the bulk of Gass's work into an overt metafiction; it is a strange little book that McCaffery regards as "a virtual casebook of literary experimentalism."[9] Upon picking up the novella, one is immediately intrigued, perhaps even shocked, by its format. As Gass has said, it is basically a creature of layout and design: it features different kinds and colors of paper, photography, many different styles of type, various genres of literature—from drama and pornography to cartoons and comic books—and has no pagination.[10] The book is a loose system, a kind of handbook or encyclopedia of many ideas; all the seemingly disparate elements, nevertheless, manage to blend together to make up a totality in the familiar manner of William Gass.

The unifying schema of the work is the extension of the metaphor of fictional language as lovemaking, the literary text as female, the reader as male. Lyrical and often driven by a bouncing meter, the prose of the work, in looping fashion, does indeed call attention to itself structurally, attempting to draw the reader's mind to the words themselves and away from the message beyond the words (quite difficult, in this case, given the competition from the strong extraliterary, visual statement of theme). Gass's professional interest in the philosophical nature of language adds yet another dimension to the self-conscious intellectuality of the work. Although *Willie Masters'* winds a little wide of Gass's usual path and makes him appear to be indeed a skater on one galosh, it is still a representative specimen of his style and wit.

"Rings on my belly where men have set down drinks"

The principal criticism that William Gass himself makes regarding *Willie Masters' Lonesome Wife* is that it fails to make the visual effects "sound" adequately.[11] In trying to make the point that language is like making love and that a book, a novelistic concept, is like a woman—a woman made of paper, ink, and glue—Gass has pushed too far away from the words themselves. Ironically, he has made such a valiant attempt to direct the reader to see the book as book that he has succeeded too well. That is to say that the writer has exceeded the primacy of the alphabetic and has therefore done what he set out to rail against: he has made the reader look beyond the words for meaning, for the "idea" that the author strives for so blatantly. Gass, discussing *Willie Masters' Lonesome Wife,* has stated that the ideas in the book turned out to be nothing but disembodied concepts—tricks that catch the reader's attention but that do not really reach artistic fulfillment. The principal fault is, to repeat, a failure to make the visual material sound properly.[12]

Although Gass, in this book, cannot be justly accused of abandoning sound,[13] visual techniques, like those shared by many of the more radical experimenters, prevail. The uninhibited photography, for instance, seems (in a kind of typically sixties way) to force the text into the desired metaphorical equation of book equals woman and reading fiction equals sexual intercourse. The title-page material is superimposed on a frontal photograph of a nude woman whose breasts, navel, and pelvic area are centrally placed on the pages. This little mock-porn slap-in-the-face in one way echoes Ron Sukenick's exhortations about waking up the phlegmatic reader, the reader who has been lulled into accepting fiction as real, dreaming in a fantasy world. Sukenick, like Federman and Gass, on occasion, likes to think of himself as getting tough with his audience, "banging them" with reality, the reality that fiction is not the world.[14] In this same spirit of radical truculence, the picture of the nude woman temporarily disallows any word-induced fantasy; we see in graphic detail what fictional characterization would have to leave out. Literary characters like Babs Masters are, as Gass says, "mostly empty canvas" (*FFL,* 45), often without certain body parts. If the woman in the picture is supposed to be Babs, we can verify that her parts are all there. Is the nude in the photograph a balance, a foil, a syzygy for the word-created Babs inside the book? Is placing the picture of a real woman at the beginning of the book the ultimate juxtaposition, the great silent philosophical lesson of the work? Or is it merely a hip, sixties amateurism of Gass's? I think a bit of both shines through the boldness of this format.

At any rate, the reader, having seen the front of the naked woman, might well wonder if she has a backside; he turns immediately to the final page and discovers yes, there it is, the rear view of the same woman. In following his curiosity, he has done what linear fiction, so-called realist fiction, tries to prevent: he has neglected to progress methodically through the book, from sentence to sentence, dutifully following the management of a contrived, mechanistic time order; he has rebelliously turned to the back page in order to discover the totality of the concept.

Before the reader may enter the paper woman from the front, however, he must once again be reminded about the propinquity of "cunt . . . to . . . concept" and his obligation as participant in this activity "to enter both with joy" (Fourth). His reminder is again photographic: the same naked woman appears on the page where the printed text begins; this time she is eating the first letter, the serpentine sibilant, the *s* that starts the first word, "she." The "message" in this "medium" is apparently that, conjuring up McLuhan, the "medium is the message." The picture of a real woman eating words must be both graphically deceptive (an image on paper that makes the viewer think he is seeing reality, the ultimate lie that Gass decries) and fictionally authentic (purely a creature of words). The author has it both ways with equal intensity. The text-woman is what she eats; she is nourished by, is made up of, words. "She" must somehow point to Babs Masters, Willie's wife, the narrator of the story, the story itself. The photographic woman is merely one extremity of the spectrum of art, the antithesis of the fictional Babs (who is "the imagination imagining itself imagine" [First]); the nude represents the failure of imagination to imagine itself imagining that negates fictional rendering. Only characters invoked through language allow us, according to Gass, to insert at a signal our own "visual memories" for the words; as language becomes more precise in its definition of an object, the less chance it has to be included in our mental picture book (*FFL,* 45). The total visualization of the photograph, therefore, since it obviously exceeds in clarity even the most precise verbal description, is the exact opposite of imagination and of art.

The bona fide Babs, however, materializes directly from the words between the coversheets. She *is* the novel that she narrates, the metafictional object, what Sukenick calls an encyclopedic multiplicity, a concrete technological structure, a box in a comic strip, a jigsaw puzzle, "a cloudburst of fragmented events."[15] The movement, the plot of the story, coincides precisely with Babs's sex act; her mind races to and fro as she submits to the lovemaking of one Phil Gelvin, the stereotypical passionless and unappreciative sex partner.

To signal and emphasize the various stages of intercourse and Babs's accompanying ruminations, the paper used in the novel changes texture and color throughout the text. This organizational device, growing naturally out of the almost unnoticeable shifts in Babs's thought patterns as she makes love, controverts the standard book divisions imposed from outside the organic structure of the narrative.[16] Experimentation with the physical shape of the novel, itself an expression of exasperation with the conventions of publishing in general, took some bizarre turns in sixties and seventies metafiction. Raymond Federman, author of a puzzle-novel called *Double or Nothing,* expresses this radical disaffection with ordinary books: "the whole traditional, conventional, fixed, and boring method of reading a book must be questioned, challenged, demolished . . . and the space itself in which writing takes place must be changed. That space, the page (and the book made of pages), must acquire new dimensions, new shapes, new relations in order to accommodate the new writing. And it is within this transformed topography of writing, from this new paginal (rather than grammatical) syntax that the reader will discover his freedom in relation to the process of reading a book, in relation to language and fiction."[17] Such radical rhetoric actually reached the fruition of practice: Marc Saporta published a novel in a box so that the pages could be constantly rearranged by the reader; other novels were written on billboards, globes, sidewalks, and videotape. Still, even the most extreme of the innovators, like Katz and Federman, whose books, because of their outrageous formats, are extremely difficult to read, at least numbered their pages. Gass, in this confusing but truly revolutionary extension of textual trope, has outdone even them.

The first pages of the story of Babs Masters (in the original edition) are inscribed on thin blue paper. The color and the texture suggest coolness, cerebration, and a more or less ordered remembrance of past events.[18] *On Being Blue,* Gass's philosophical meditation on that color and its relation to the erotic nature of language, bears directly on the first section. Blue, states Gass, is perhaps the color of reality itself. Luminescent and indicative of life, the color blue is also the hue of death: "There is that lead-like look. There is the lead itself, and all those bluey hunters, thieves, those pigeon flyers who relieve roofs of the metal, and steal the pipes too. There's the blue pill that is the bullet's end, the nose, the plum, the blue whistler, and there are all the bluish hues of death."[19]

The color blue, for Gass, has a sexual, pornographic connotation. Gass describes a photograph, a "blue picture," of a naked girl standing in front of the family trailer: "embarrassed breasts and frightened triangle, vacant stare . . . stringy hair, head out of plumb, smile like a scratch across her face . . . my friends brought her image with them from their camping trip" (*OBB,* 8).

Taken and sold by the girl's father, it is a quintessentially amateur (formless) rendering of the reality of the female body (indeed of reality itself). Gass wonders how much the father got for the photo (*OBB*, 8), what value it could have beyond the titillation of the basest, most undernourished sensibilities, the untutored lust of a boy getting his first glimpse of an unclothed girl: "My sensations were as amateur as her photo" (*OBB*, 8). What the inexperienced Gass remembered most about the picture was a weed growing between the steps of the trailer. The weed unites the unposed, unpruned nature of the piece of pornography with the bluishness of death, the color of lead, bullet lead, that emphasizes absence, absence of art and of life: "Loneliness, emptiness, worthlessness, grief . . . each is an absence in us" (*OBB*, 11–12). The weed, an unmanaged, wild vitality that left to itself takes over the most carefully planned garden, is a symbol of "sexuality . . . dangerously Dionysian" (*OBB*, 8). "Nowhere," says Gass, "do we need order more than at an orgy" (*OBB*, 8). Just as direct sunlight must be mediated by a parasol, so the starkness of objective reality (particularly as manifested in sex and death) needs to be filtered by form: "What is form, in any case, but a bumbershoot held up against the absence of all cloud?" (*OBB*, 8) This photo, then, and that on the title page of *Willie Masters' Lonesome Wife* both stand for one of the "common methods by which sex gains an entrance into literature . . . the commonest . . . the most brazen: the direct depiction of sexual material" (*OBB*, 10–11). The photographic image of Babs Masters eating letters off blue paper thus juxtaposes the infantile directness of pornography with the subtlety and depth of love expressed as linguistic form: "the use of language like a lover . . . not the language of love, but the love of language, not matter, but meaning, not what the tongue touches, but what it forms, not lips and nipples, but nouns and verbs" (*OBB*, 11).

The low-key, deliberate language of the blue section is nevertheless sophisticated and diversified. To achieve the intricacy of a musical score, the impression that snatches of language can be sounded out simultaneously or at different "speeds" and "pitches,"[20] Gass folds in another innovation: the alternation of type styles to match the alternation of point of view and voice. Many experimenters resort to this method of destroying narrative linearity: some, like Katz (*The Exaggerations of Peter Prince*), have several story lines going on the same page. The blue-paged section of *Willie Masters'* features three simultaneous sources of story, three concurrent voices, that are differentiated by roman, italic, and boldface type, respectively. This section can thus be read in two ways: one may read in the usual way, from top to bottom, left to right, perceiving the three tiers of Babs's musings; or one may read all the material presented in one mode of type, a method that requires skipping from page to page and then going back to read the other two strands of narrative. The first level, printed in italics, is a third-person account of Babs's youthful sexual activity, especially an encounter with a conductor on a train when she was really just a child, a "rehearsal" for her life as a loose woman. The second, in roman letters, is from Babs's first-person point of view, the standard autobiographical mode. In this print format, Babs comments on the names of body parts, noses, penises of her lovers; this naming corresponds to the narration of her youthful romances in italics. The roman type also allows her to comment on her own large breasts. Tying into the initial photo, and by extension into the photo of the naked girl in *On Being Blue,* Babs relates how her own father had leered at her pectoral development: "A regular dairy, my daddy always said" (First). He, as a counterpart to the father in *On Being Blue* who sold the picture of his nude daughter, is also the first in her long line of masculine admirers who could see only the most obvious, the sexual, side of her nature.

In roman type, Babs also discusses her literary nature, not as character, but as the fictive process, literature itself. She dreams and makes things up, like Madame Bovary; but, unlike Emma, she does not die in the book—and of course cannot die in the world. As a book on the shelf, she is immortal (First). The reader, like a lover, finishes his coital relationship, but Babs is still there, used, lonely, but not dead; she is not a character who dies within the superstructure of the novel: she is the novel and therefore superior to the mortal reader in every way. This is the beginning of the long monologue about being and not being with regard to fiction. It is a prolonged discourse by Babs on Babs, the embodiment of literature, a mirror that "endlessly unimages itself, yet is none the less an image" (First). There is even a page printed mirror-backwards, the literal incorporation of the idea.

The boldface lines carry out a kind of recurrent beat in the background, like a drone note (a technique, as we have seen, put to good use in *Omensetter's Luck*). This note is the intermittent reiteration of the metaphor of saliva, the basic and less than sanitary matter of physical seduction, the drink of amorous transubstantiation, the "sweet wine of love" (First). The eucharist of love and literature transforms men (readers) from what they really are to what they could be in theory. Women (novels) love these men in theory, in their "aura" of humanity; whores like Babs become inured to the sickening array of bodies with rancid breaths, various decompositions and deformities (First); they, like soldiers, get used to the "untidiness," fears, and deaths of their fellows (First); they become more inclusive, more tolerant, more human than most of humanity. Like feet, they are used unmercifully, and therefore are candidates for humility and a "saintly" kind of love (First). Those objects that are the least appreciated, used for some other purpose, like David Jones's *Anathemata,* are those most worthy of becoming objects of veneration.

If readers slow down and allow themselves to see words for what they really are, the way Babs wants her lovers to "read" her, they would realize just how intractable language really is, how absorbent it is: the word "screw," for example, is not at all accurate, for, as Babs observes, intercourse, from the man's perspective, is more like hammering nails (First). Like Barthelme's Snow White, Babs regrets that words have become so trivialized, so overworked that they have lost their vigor. Babs feels the "terror of terminology," the dearth of effective, exciting words (First).

As Babs's passion rises, the color of the pages changes into an oily olive, the paper becomes thicker and more highly textured, and the typography and graphic layout of the pages occasionally verge on outlandishness. Parallel to Babs's rising level of coital excitement, the text of this section varies wildly in form. Some pages begin with small boldface type, but at the bottom the letters have ballooned to four or five times the size of that at the top of the page. The use of footnotes to comment upon, indeed to add substantially to the text, has been a hallmark of modernist poets like Pound, Eliot, and Jones. Gass parodies this practice by footnoting with asterisks. At first used merely to mark notes offering information about such topics as Locke's semiotics and to supply stage directions for the intercalated minidrama (about a man finding his penis in his breakfast bun), the asterisks in this section soon become absurdly omnipresent. At one point, giant asterisks take over an entire page, floating like snow flakes in the blankness of the paper. The text (Babs) applauds the gratuitous use of these peculiar inked stars: they are "the prettiest things in print" (Second).

The most interesting and functional print effect in this section is the illusion of undulation, of being on a roller coaster, of bouncing up and down—a sensation produced by selective distortion of letters. This apparent bending, stretching, and twisting of the words on the page enhances Babs's passionate insistence, in flagrante delicto, that she is nothing but a "mimic of movement in silent readers . . . a column of air moving up and down" (Second), the coituslike undulation of a string of words on paper. The clever arrangement of paper and ink, however, makes the reader come very close to experiencing palpably the moving up and down of a column of air or, under certain conditions, of writhing bodies in passion. The torsion of the print, if one can escape without a headache or a queasiness in the stomach, leads to a rolling (visually and verbally) monologue on the relationship between death and art. The beauty of Babs's fictional language, which is facilitated by the serpentine, twisted, wallowy letters that she has ingested like "licorice," is, on the other hand, not quite as impervious to destruction as she boasts. The ink-licorice of written language, after all, is the invention of that same "unfortunate, made-so-differently-so-disastrously, dying" animal, the human being, whose breastbone is bone and not the sound "ul" (as in "lull," the stoppage of being that the text suffers after the reader no longer reads) as is the sternum of Babs (Second). Babs, like all systems of language, must be written, read, or spoken by humans, must have commonality with people of flesh and blood, and therefore participate, as Wittgenstein says, in exterior meaning, some "out-of-work meaning, an unruly and maddened metaphor" (Second). Private communication systems cannot exist as language;[21] Babs, therefore, is "not so good" as she imagines herself imagining that she is; she has "caught a claw"; something "has bitten a hole in [her] lining"; it is the "lull that's inside me come evening" (Second).

The red section continues in the hard-driving, three-part stream of thought that narrows into precise philosophical analysis of language. The boldface section keeps up the background reiteration of Babs's nature as two-pronged being: "significant sound . . . the language of imagination" (Third). The roman lines discuss the nature of words and Platonic forms (Third). The italicized piece of each red page alternates with a section printed in capitals; the italics perpetuate the dialogued, dramatized musings of Babs about words and perceptions; the capitals sing out a long list of items, associated (as in the beginning of the first section pages) with a poker game, and thereby demonstrating what Gass considers one of the five ways of introducing sexuality in literature: displacement (*OBB*, 42–43).

The reading-sexual encounter ends on the last page of the third section with very large letters proclaiming that the affair has ended in a double way ("You've been had, from start to finish"). Either the reader-lover has cheated and skipped a large portion of the text to get to this terminus, or he has pushed ahead with the process with dogged determination: either the reader (Gelvin) has been content "to sink so suddenly from soft to bony . . . to kiss an ear if followed by the belly" or he has played the "literalist at loving," plugging "ahead like the highway people's line machine, straight over hill and dale, unwavering and ready, in a single stripe of kiss and covering" (last page, third section). Babs does not expect the text, herself, to have been read the proper way; that would be too much to hope for: "Really, did you read this far? puzzle your head? turn the pages this and that, around about?" (last page, third section)

The last part, an eloquent and straightforward summation of the "idea" of *Willie Masters'*, is printed on high quality white paper, paper that calls to mind formal reports and expensive publications. The prose is dignified and without gimmick, reflecting Babs's (postcoital) postreading sobriety and lack of erotic stimulation. Babs's mood is philosophical and her words are measured. Unhappy with the unimaginative lover, Gelvin, who has just left her (put her away on the shelf), she expresses her hope of finding in the next customer a great mind with whom she might have true literary intercourse— perhaps Gelvin's brother.

To match the whiteness of the paper, the text is frequently interlaced with words that suggest light: "sterile star . . . glow . . . moon . . . daylight . . . diamonds interlaced and wound with silver flowers bursting into bloom like bombs," and so forth (Fourth). Likewise, to parallel the blackness of the ink on the handsome white surface, some words and phrases deliberately evoke darkness: "blacken the stage . . . passed behind clouds . . . night frightens . . . dull, bleak busy walls . . . covers . . . like craven cuttlefish, cloud ink around me . . . make a start against the darkness . . . dim figures like the zodiac's" (Fourth). But the balance is tipped in favor of the white, signifying the chastity and the emptiness of Babs on the shelf. The large photo (First) of the nude eating a block with a letter on it has been, in the white section (Fourth), replaced by a picture of the same woman in the fetal position with her face and her private parts hidden. She has returned to a luminescent (as opposed to the sensually colored) presexual state. Her lights have failed to illuminate the inept reader; the laser (light-heat) of the text has not done its work in cutting away the crust of customary expectations; the book has contracted again into itself, into a seed or kernel of extraordinary potential that awaits the fertilization of the next reader: "I should, had he not worn his celloguard, have been but seven months to bud, a week to bloom, and three more days to fruiting" (Fourth).

Like Sterne and Joyce, who played with and parodied typographical commonplaces,[22] Gass presents in this work a little history (through samples of print and paper) of European writing and the printing business: handwritten cursive, Gothic script, musical notation, late nineteenth-century typeface, stencil, advertising block, and newspaper title and headline all emphasize developments in the profession of producing printed pages.[23] The periodic insertion of these graphical scraps from the history of printing serves as yet another reminder that books are the offspring of other books, that there is an undeniable dialogue between one text and another as well as between literary generations. Literature, like human life, has a genealogy; each set of youngsters is automatically set at odds with the preceding elders. As an inheritor of the technological advances in media, Gass finds both irritation with their present uses, particularly in the publishing world, and delight at the potential they afford the artist to express himself. The extraordinary features of this book, made possible by cumulative advances in the bookmaker's craft since the sixteenth century, combine to create and reinforce in the mind a vision of a woman, a text, totally made of ink and paper.

The Art of Reading

Not only is the graphic layout of *Willie Masters'* puzzling and often difficult to decipher; reading in the normal manner becomes more obstacle-bound, more of a challenge, as we move along in the text, especially through the dense undergrowth of the olive and red pages. Making sense of the text makes greater demands on the reader, calling on his patience with gamesmanship in the Nabokovian or Borgesian sense, forcing him, ironically, by means of the habit of reading in straight lines, into traps and dead ends that make him suddenly aware that he is not reading in the traditional way at all. In the olive section (Second), for instance, appears a little trick predicated upon the natural inclination of most people to go from one thing to another and the normal curiosity in all of us to find out what is going on; this device leads into a deceptive labyrinth; the usual response to this kind of tomfoolery is to abandon the book, at least as a conventional novel, and treat it more like a handbook, a dictionary, a book of tables, an atlas, or a guidebook. That is what happens, and that is the point. The reader discovers an asterisk that marks a footnote clearly visible at the bottom of the page (the same system alluded to above); since it is merely a wardrobe note to the intercalated skit followed by a seemingly unrelated blurb about the family of Napoleon, he skips it and proceeds with the text. But he is hooked, because the next note is not located on the same page. The reader-turned-sleuth now has to thumb ahead in the text, breaking the linear train of thought that he may have acquired thus far. The note relates Locke's ideas about universals and particulars to the discovery of the penis in the roll (the topic of the skit). This discourse is a bit long for a note, but it makes sense. The reader regains his confidence in the author; he will undoubtedly read the next footnote. This time the text of the miniplay contains a simile comparing the bald heads of some men in the audience with white tulips bobbing in the wind. The note points out that the expression "bald bastards" is "a cliché of course" (Second) and the fourth note proclaims that the simile is a fake image. The fourth footnote is a note to the third footnote; the fifth note is a note to the fourth note. There is, however, another fourth footnote which ironically drones on about "natural writing," and the world as a "nest of contrivance" (Second). The "of course" in the footnote is a "literary stutter" to keep the eyes of the reader going down the page. At the end of the page, Babs reveals the point of this game. She gloats to the reader about her just-demonstrated power over him, the power to make his eyes move down into an "oily" precinct at the bottom of the page (Second).

This clever little stratagem demonstrates the wrongheadedness that meta-fictionists like Gass see as the root of deception and stagnation in conventional novels. All verbal communication, especially imaginative writing, is based on a system of fabrications about the real world that, although having the appearance of objectivity about things, really are only subjective manipulations of words that reveal an aspiration to know the world. These attempts are necessary in order for people to organize the happenings of their lives into some structure of meaning, to regularize an existence that for the most part is chaotic. Language places an artificial grid on an unstable field; fiction attempts to play a game within the limits of the grid, and part of the game is to make use of the instability of the ground supposedly normalized by language. The problem for fiction makers is that readers, in their passion to discover a permanent ordering of things in life, expect to proceed logically from one point to another, discovering the secrets of every mechanism, and getting answers that they assume are hidden within the structure of sentences and paragraphs just as they expect to find reliable knowledge hidden in the static, mechanistic universe of the positivist.[24]

Finding that not every fiction is necessarily a detective story that leads to a solution, or that not every footnote illuminates the text of a story or an argument, is a shock, and that shock is what Gass seems to attempt in the above segment. If literature does not lead the reader along to some conclusion or solution, then the language of literature must have some purpose other than utility. That other purpose is what William Gass calls to our attention. It is the opposite of what most people read books for, to get the "gist" (*HW*, 226), to look through the words to the "bottom line," to reach the "climax without the bother of buildup or crescendo" (*HW*, 223).

Willie Masters' Lonesome Wife asserts that there is a way to read that is more consonant with what written discourse, if it is good, really is. Gass in this book tries to force his readers, accustomed as all of us are to getting through books, to slow down and "perform the text, say, sing, shout the words," at least read it silently the way we taste wine: "We sip. We savor" (*HW*, 227–28). Just as Babs laments the haste of Gelvin to get done and leave her, Gass deplores "literal learning" that impatient readers try to get from books, particularly finely wrought books of fiction. This essay-novella is a much more elegant statement of metafictional aspirations than the works of most of the other experimental writers of the sixties and seventies.

The metafictional impulse has been to make sure that the works themselves, the outcomes of paper and ink, the agglutinations of words and files of words, register their meaning in the mind. Barthelme is so preoccupied with the act of paying attention to his text that he gives the reader a test in the middle of *Snow White*. One of the test items asks if the work has metaphysical dimension. If there is such dimension the reader is asked to discuss it in twenty-five words or less. Another asks the reader whether he would like a war.[25]

The most extravagant writing by a practitioner of this "disruptive" fiction is Raymond Federman's *Double or Nothing*. This novel, or "novelty," features almost every conceivable way to compel its reader to disengage himself from the conventional manner of reading a text, to call attention to its made-up-ness, its alienation from real or utilitarian written language. The beginning, labeled "THIS IS NOT THE BEGINNING," begins in the traditional way, with the initial words of fairy tales, "Once upon a time."[26] The beginning page, marked as such, is ringed with a sentence that forms a margin by reading successively from left to right, top to bottom, right to left, then back up the page from bottom to top. There are pages with nothing but one word written over five hundred times in the shape of a cross. There is a page with the diagram of a set of stairs with the words "UP AND DOWN" written over and over on the "steps." There are swastikas, footnotes, grocery lists, instructions for teeth brushing, and even an index of topics ("In the girls' room . . . The smell and the ass of certain women as prominent features of their femininity"[27]) at the end. Federman achieves what he advocates in his essay (which introduces his book) on metafiction: "the most striking aspects of the new fiction will be its semblance of disorder and its deliberate incoherency."[28]

William Gass, too, seems to have been infected by this extremist contagion of sixties disorderliness. *Willie Masters',* in its unorthodox and campy presentation of "concept as cunt," succeeds in making the reader hesitate, suffer the little planned shocks, wonder about the story that is not really a story, become confused, and ultimately, in most cases, lose interest. For those who can remain patient with the games and effects, however, there are, as in practically all of Gass's works, the undeniable attractiveness of his style and the depth of his thought.

Language and Philosophy

The dual nature of language, sound and sense, presents problems other than purely artistic ones. Language, because it is relentlessly intertwined with thinking and being, occupies this work and all of Gass's writing to a substantial degree. Babs's philosophical ruminations about words add a technical, theoretical dimension to the book, justifying its being called an "essay-novella."[29] This fusion of fiction and essay, at least the way that Gass brings it about, is the stamp of originality that *Willie Masters'* bears, and, as I have stated, is what separates this work from its shallow counterparts in the avant-garde fiction of the sixties.

The level of Babs's thinking that takes the form of minidrama or skit enters the arena of the perennial polemic regarding words and ideas, language and knowledge. Ivan realizes that what he has found in his bun is not his nose, but some other thing—and that other thing is "an unmistakable general idea" that registers in his brain as a penis, his penis. This recognition, since it is a theatrical demonstration of the way the mind works, deserves (the text is at least part essay) a lengthy footnote. The footnote allows Gass the metafictional pleasure of commenting directly and philosophically upon his own work; he can enter its controlling concept himself as can a reader with a knowledge of basic epistemology, a subject that the footnote briefly summarizes. The reference to the second book of Locke's *Concerning Human Understanding* is a perfect start for the beginning of a disquisition on the problematic relationship of words and the world. Modern speculation about signs and meaning amounts to variations on the basic theme planted by Immanuel Kant in the late eighteenth century.

The Kantian revolution in philosophy set the stage for a dramatic turn away from the rationalism of the Enlightenment and a turn toward a rebirth of faith and feeling that was to characterize the romantic movement. In order to understand Kant, one must start, as Babs starts, with the notions of John Locke (1632–1704). Following the lead of Francis Bacon, Locke continued to turn reason (the chief tool of philosophical inquiry and the instrument that would allow science and mathematical logic to solve all mankind's problems) upon itself in the attempt to discover the nature and workings of the mind. This inward-looking inadvertently became the seed of what would become the romantic outlook, an unlikely flower that would blossom from this same root over a hundred years later. In between, of course, came the harsh rationality of the eighteenth century; but even in the midst of the Enlightenment occurred the working out of a fundamental criticism of reason as the dominant force in epistemology. Many theologians of the day, worried that faith would be lost in a God whose existence could not be proved empirically, resorted to the position that knowledge of the world was innate, present at birth and prior to experience. Locke challenged this notion. His idea was that all knowledge has its origin in the senses, and that without the senses there could be nothing in the mind. At birth, a person's mind is a clean slate, a sheet of paper that can be written upon only by the pen of experience that moves as sight, hearing, touch, smell, and taste operate on the objects and happenings of the world. Experience through the senses, in its manifold workings on the mental tabula rasa, produces memory; by means of memory, ideas register in the mind. According to a straightforward reading of Locke, as Babs (or Gass) provides in the footnote, mentality is nothing but "ideas being taken from particular things," and words "stand as outward marks for our internal ideas" (Second). Because the whole process of cognition is based on the mental organization of ideas that arise from experience predicated in turn upon sensual perception of material objects only, Locke's epistemology is materialistic.

Naming, this assigning of words for things, is, as it was for Locke, the focal point for the preoccupation with thinking and expression of thought in Gass's writing and in modern philosophy. To avoid the impossible task of giving a name to each individual object that stirs the senses and registers its existence in the network of thought, the mind is obliged to generalize, to group objects into categories: "if every particular idea that we take in, masticate, and swallow down, should have a distinct name, names must be endless . . . to prevent this, the mind makes the particular ideas, received from particular objects, to become general like the spread of a disease . . . destroying the trees" (Second). Such destruction of particular things by naming them is "called abstraction, sometimes love, and always the art of writing" (Second).

Bishop George Berkeley (1684–1753) subsequently refuted a materialist theory of knowledge and turned Locke's arguments against themselves. Berkeley stated that since, as Locke said, mind arises from the sensual perception of matter only and arranges that matter into its own configurations, we know nothing of matter itself, only our perception of it. Therefore, matter exists only as a mental form. Things are nothing but a collection of perceptions, sensations sorted and analyzed by the mind. Does a flame exist, for instance, if there is no eye to see its light, no nose to smell its smoke, no hand to feel its heat, no ear to hear its hiss and crackle? Berkeley would say no; that a flame's existence is merely a mental construct. The bishop's opposition to materialism led David Hume (1711–76) to question the "materiality" of the mind as well. The mind, like matter, is nothing but a wad of memories and ideas that can be perceived randomly without any organizing agent such as mind or soul; "mind" and "soul" are only words that abstract these series of thoughts and emotions into artificial categories. Likewise, science cannot rely on necessity, natural law. It is impossible to observe laws, or causes; it is possible only to observe effects and summarize them into some kind of lore. But nothing happens according to law or necessity; we infer causes for effects but cannot know any rule for sequences of events. Only mathematical concepts are incontrovertible because they are tautological; that is, mathematical statements merely replicate themselves. Five plus five equals ten because five plus five is just another way of saying ten. Ten is a reiteration, not an effect of five plus five. Science can only compute and observe sequences in phenomena. There is no mind, no law, to organize perception. Gass summarizes Hume's philosophy in linguistic terms: "The Humean sentence will reduce objects to their qualities, maintain an equality between them by using non-subordinating conjunctions, be careful not to confuse emotion and reflection with perception, but at the same time will allow their presence in the same onward flow. Everywhere, Hume makes his world out of lists and collections" (*FFL*, 15). One may list but not order the list. Thus, just as Berkeley had deconstructed matter, so Hume exploded mind. Philosophy had reached an untenable extreme; it had immolated itself in the fire of reason. Kant sought to resuscitate it through a brilliant act of synthesis: he taught that to think is to order, that a list is automatically an ordering.

For Kant, and for latter-day philosophers whom we may label Neo-Kantians (Idealists—including William Gass), there is an order inherent in the structure of the mind that Kant calls "pure reason," as opposed to the adulterated and twisted, much less than perfect path to knowledge offered by the senses. Kant opposes Locke and Hume in his contention that knowledge is not totally gleaned from sensational contact with the world; there is pre-experiential knowledge, a knowledge that Kant calls a priori, that allows for absolute truth, absolute knowledge, and science. Mind comes fully equipped to organize the chaos of experiential world into thought; it is not merely an abstraction of sense data nor is it a blank tablet for sense data to write upon. Kant's concept of mind synthesizes the materialism of Locke with the ancient idealism of Plato. One level of thinking consists of the subjection of sensation to the ordering of the two modes of intellection: time and space. Kant calls this first stage transcendental estheticism, estheticism used here in its original meaning of feeling, sensation. The second, logic, is the subjection of perceptions, conditioned already by time and space, to his "categories," forms inherent in the mind. This absolutism, however, is paradoxically tied inextricably to common human experience, to the way human beings view things. Reality for Kant has an undeniable existence as "things in themselves," but these things cannot be experienced: they can only be conceived in the mind, for their journey to perception (stimulus to sensation to perception to concept) changes them into mental constructs peculiar to human beings. Both things in the world and the human mind are necessary components of the world: things contribute stimuli that eventually become concepts and people contribute the necessary mental molding. The familiar example of the placing at arm's length of a coin on a table at which one is seated illustrates this double nature of things: the coin, although round, presents itself to the eye as an ellipse. Because of our a priori notion of the roundness of coins, we still perceive the coin as round, even though as a stimulus, it is elliptical. Thus, any attempt of reason to escape the tight ring of stimuli, of appearance, and into the realm of things in themselves, an unknowable domain, is ultimately impossible.[30]

This desire to reach the impossible world of things is the philosophical platform of Gass's fiction. Babs, symbolic of the concept that can never really be experienced as a material object (except as the paper and ink of her existence), is a phenomenon, an appearance, knowable only by the imagination that can arrange the stimuli supplied by the words and visual effects of her "being" into a mental construct that has its own reality. Her being, then, depends, as she says constantly, upon the power of the reader's mind to make her up out of the cluster of verbal stimuli that she spews forth. Just as the sex act requires equal participation from both partners, so also does the act of knowing require both the object's stimuli and the organizing human mind. To reach her ontological fullness, Babs must have an adept conceiver. The search for such a reader and the determination of how he reads when he picks up a book constitute the theme of this unusual work. *Willie Masters' Lonesome Wife* is therefore, in addition to being a comprehensive metaphor of fiction writing and reading, a philosophical allegory. The quest for elusive things, transferred from space to time, the search for historical "fact," is the theme of Gass's novel-in-progress, "The Tunnel."

Chapter Five

"The Tunnel": "A Path through Time and a Pile of Debris"

William Gass has spent more than fifteen years writing what he hopes will be his ideal novel, a work that generates its own form, a totally self-referential fiction built upon a compelling, even explosive theme.[1] Unlike *Omensetter's Luck,* which Gass considers to have been a more rigidly planned work,[2] "The Tunnel" is fragmentary and ruled by one all-encompassing metaphor, the attempted extermination of the Jews and other unwanted peoples by the Nazis. This metaphor includes the exploration of the nature and uses of history as history relates to remembering, being, and time. The novel, published as a series of short stories in literary journals, is still unfinished despite Gass's repeated promises of a termination date: the last public announcement of the projected advent (of which I am aware) was made in an interview with Arthur Saltzman that appeared in Saltzman's book on Gass in 1986. Gass stated at that time that he knew how long the novel was to be and that it would be ready in about another year. That year and others have passed, but perhaps we may expect to see it in print fairly soon.

Gass has stated that "The Tunnel" has its origin in the Furber section of *Omensetter's Luck* and in "In the Heart of the Heart of the Country."[3] The narrator and main character has strong affinities with other self-buried narrators in the author's work, Israbestis Tott, for example. What Gass, after all these years of writing and rewriting his prose, has apparently found as an ideal manner of working is a combination of the incessant, compelling rhetoric of the great Furber monologues and the nonlinearity of "In the Heart."[4] The verbal gush emanates from William Frederick Kohler, a history professor whose field of specialization is Nazi Germany. The reader is expected to extract a story (based on the paradigm of Nazi mentality) from the tide of words upon which the fragments of narrative float. Kohler has just finished a book, an exhaustive study of the Holocaust titled *Guilt and Innocence in Hitler's Germany,* a book that Kohler hopes will be a monument to his scholarly achievement, his magnum opus. In the book, he has attempted to amass an overwhelming number of facts from the documents of the time; from the mountains of data, he has attempted to find some meaning for himself in the period, to find some rationale for the events, the causes as well as the effects of the so-called Final Solution. Kohler stands to incur the displeasure of many because of this book; it tends to be too cozy, too soothing, too close to the verge of forgiving the Germans for their gross inhumanity. But the reader is allowed to see very little of this work; only the beginning and the final pages of the novel will contain direct quotation from it.[5] It is the preface that Kohler writes that makes up the content of "The Tunnel"; it is the attempt to comment on the incomprehensible magnitude of the story suggested by Kohler's research that prompts his excavation of his own German roots, his own guilt about having participated even in a symbolic way in the early persecutions of the Jews (he had thrown a brick into the glass of a Jew's window on *Kristallnacht*).

The purpose of his preface is supposed to be to make some personal but academically significant comment on his work, the rigorously objective presentation of his historical theme, the guilt and the innocence of the people of the Third Reich. The manuscript and its facts, however, suggest nothing but deep subjective reverie on the part of Kohler; he takes off on a journey of remembrance of his past, recalling his childhood, his student days in Germany, his former professor, his uncle, his parents, his wife, his children, the ugly little midwestern Dust Bowl town where he grew up during the depression, his teaching career.

If Kohler is not lecturing his students or sitting in his chair, a chair that he has inherited from his mentor, his former teacher (Magus Tabor, hyperverbal and eccentric to the point of madness), he is engaged in the actual digging of a tunnel in his basement (or at least describes such an excavation in convincing detail that competes with the reality of his book).[6]

We quickly learn that this mania for "digging in" has been with Kohler since his childhood; it places him in the tradition of other Gass narrators who seek a place of safety, a protected precinct from which to observe without being seen, to be an unperceived perceiver. Ensconced unseen in his parents' bedroom, he experiences himself as "untrammeled and fountainous will . . . a presence, a force."[7] Although the young Kohler (like the young William Gass) had moved into many houses with his errant parents, he had always managed to find a protected fortress: a bush, a barn, anywhere away from the "mob's middle distance" ("Windows," 294). Everyone, especially those who have had to move frequently in childhood or who have had difficulties with parents, can easily be drawn into the tender anger expressed in these pages by "Koh." The special world of Kohler's childhood is drawn for us in deft, lyrical strokes; our sympathies are captured and made secure; Kohler seems to be so much like all lonely children who live in a world of make-believe and warm imagination despite the cold of the adult world outside the special places of refuge: the taciturn youngster built secret passageways and impenetrable rooms with his blocks, drew mazes, and, like Israbestis Tott, traced imaginary jungles, swamps, deserts, and battlefields in the weave of rugs ("Windows," 296).

And like all children, Kohler had to deal with "them," the adult world, the realm outside his tunnel. Allegiances had to be professed to the conventions of society, and even these forced affirmations of things "good for you" bring fond, if at times mordant, memories of childhood. Little William Kohler, even in relating this less than blissful part of growing up, still manages to establish a rapport with the reader, worms into the reader's sympathy, for all of us have had basically similar childhood experiences, and the remembrance of them is touching. Like Kohler, we have all told the expected trivial lies, professing to accept the public beliefs designated for children: the value of work, the beauty of a younger sister, or "each of those rules [his] father described as summing up common sense or Herbert Hoover, and every one of the so-called laws of God, Man, Nature, and the state" ("Windows," 297). Although the reader may wince slightly at the cynicism of the last prepositional phrase, he is still carried along by nostalgia, carried along into the tunnel of the narrative, and like Alice, begins to luxuriate in the swirl of images, forgetting the rabbit.

Gass has done what he has announced that he wants to do in this novel. He has made readers identify, even if just a little, with the narrator. Speaking of "The Tunnel," Gass has said that he hopes to present a questionable mentality so that it will attract his audience into an appreciation of it in the space of a reading; to "indict" the reader, in Gass's words.[8] Gass, confessing to manipulation of the reader, calls this scheme making the reader say "yes" to Kohler's persona, giving "grandeur to a shit."[9] While the blissful "unpressured seeing" ("Windows," 294) of the child in the tunnels of his making allows for great beauty, it also stimulates a dangerous disassociation; in escaping the vision, the surveillance of society, the unseen viewer substitutes his imaginary world for the daily life of ordinary human beings. Not being caged in anybody else's field of vision means that other people are "surely caught in mine" ("Windows," 294). Kohler, even in childhood "hiding out," can become dangerously contemptuous of those in his cage of vision so that when he returns to the quotidian, "where the clock ticks," he is repelled by the idea of the "common view" ("Windows," 297). Thus, Kohler, even as a child, has been totally self-consumed, dangerously at odds with ordinary life: his happiness has been to crawl inside himself and find there a private life like the solitude and self-sufficiency Jonah found in the belly of the whale ("Windows," 293).

The compulsion to escape from "the mob's middle distance" follows the professor-narrator into adulthood. Kohler tells about his fascination with student folklore having to do with a certain maintenance crawl space in the building that houses his office: reportedly, a separate life exists there, with a treasure chest of stolen examinations and students living comfortably in its confines, cooking eggs and boiling coffee on the steam pipes. There is even rumor of a coed-staffed bordello in the duct. Such is the nature and the attraction of tunnels: departure from the eyes of one's fellows or the dean makes for a world of bizarre possibilities. One of these possibilities is divinity ("Windows," 298). This same sense of divinity, this fearlessness, this freedom from oversight that their fictional superiority over life gave them, this freedom from conventional "hypocrisy," this "sincerity," is at the core of nazism: Nazis rose "as gods" from their entombment in the pettiness of middle-class life "for sainthood" ("Windows," 306). If we have been led to find Kohler attractive, we must now also see him for the "shit" that he is. There is in our identification with the protagonist (supposedly one of the objectives of realist fiction) the built-in realization that perhaps we might also be "grand shits," which, of course, we are. As Gass would put it, we have been "bail-tailed."

The structural nature of tunnels, empty spaces supported by the surrounding edifice of various materials, allows the imagination unlimited freedom from both the prying eyes of the world and the moral-enforcing vision of society. One day Kohler actually unscrews the cover of a maintenance tunnel with a dime and crawls inside. He enters the shaft on many occasions as though he had somehow to ritualize his verbal tunnels with some kind of physical activity. During one passage in the duct, he gets stuck; he can neither retreat nor advance for a time. Like his basement tunnel digging, this tunneling reifies his burning desire to tunnel out or into an impossible-to-reach place. Once again, the narrator has given physical properties to the imaginary tunnel in his mind. He is, as are all Gass's narrators and even Gass himself, a prisoner of the book, of a fictional construct that commands a total commitment of energy and at the same time fences out the world. This, then, is the directing metaphor, the trope for the text that will allow for a departure from traditional linear narrative. The book itself is a tunnel; writing a book is digging a tunnel.[10]

Gass wants the reader of this novel to have an experience that will be a temporary ersatz for his daily consciousness. We are supposed to share the sensation of enclosure, feel ourselves surrounded by armed guards. Coming under the spell of words fired at us by the narrator, we are supposed to try to dig our way into them and out of them; we must sort the shards of meaning and make our own piles from this verbal debris. Reading the novel, thus, parallels what Kohler does (or talks about doing) in his basement. The reader, imitating Kohler (German for "miner"), becomes a miner himself, making a hole moment after moment or day after day and disposing of the dirt. The reader burrows into a text that is "both a path through time and a pile of debris."[11] Kohler, likewise, digs into his past (having failed in his own book to penetrate the past of Nazi Germany) and from the material of his own life, packs and molds around the reader a kind of fictional dirt, forming thus the walls of a tunnel, the tunnel of the novel. In Kohler's "referential life," he takes dirt out, but in the making of his book, he pours this dirt in and molds it. He builds, therefore, one tunnel from the outside and another one from the inside, the latter the location of the reader's imagination.[12]

"The Great Tabor's Own Chair"

Kohler's "referential life" stands for the accepted and expected convention of action in a piece of fiction: that a character "do something."[13] As we have come to expect in Gass, this action, digging, is a part of the central metaphor and therefore a symbolic act, an act having an allegorical function. The allegory here is the making of a tunnel as analogous to the making of a novel. Tunnel burrowing, as Gass points out, is both a taking out—and by extension to archaeology and then to history, an attempt to uncover the leavings of the past—and a problem regarding what to do with what is unearthed. Thus, Kohler's digging in his basement, whether he does it or imagines himself doing it, is merely another way of expressing the same things that go on as he sits in Tabor's chair, a silent and smoothly swiveling magic carpet that allows him to put into practice what the great Tabor had taught him: that the historian may vanish at any given moment into the past, that through words and the mind that constructs them (and is in turn constructed by them), the writer-thinker may find any one of many passages that lead back into time. In the first three sentences of the section entitled "Mad Meg," Gass through Kohler sets about immediately to demonstrate this basic historical process (paralleling the constant backward-stretching ruminations of Israbestis Tott, Furber, and the narrator of "In the Heart"): Kohler sits in Tabor's chair, a chair that he has shipped from Germany, and thinks. Immediately he is transported in his mind to the lecture hall at the university. The abrupt temporal shift from Kohler in the chair to Kohler in the lecture hall of the German university where he sat as Tabor's student is representative of the many dramatic breaks of this kind; this shift emblemizes the central theme of "The Tunnel," the desire to unite past and present. This desire promulgates a verbal fusing of the past and the present: history becomes a matter of linguistic "cobbling," putting data together artificially, that forces history, under strict scrutiny, to reveal itself not as fact, but as mere rhetorical prestidigitation.[14]

For Magus "Mad Meg" Tabor, as well as for Kant and latter-day idealists, facts are at least in part creatures made of concepts, the mind's ordering of perceptions that grow out of sensation. Facts, therefore, are not coequal with things in the "real world" (unknowable phenomena); facts are not products of nature but of the mind which itself is a part of nature; and although we hunger after facts and desire to know them directly, we can never get their full meaning because in the attempt to know them, we create them ourselves. So historians who tunnel into the facts of the past are left with nothing but dirt and debris; they must pack that dirt and debris around some focus, and this focal point is a readership for whom they write their books or an audience to whom they lecture.

William Gass has said that he chooses a name for a character and then lets the character grow outward from the name.[15] The name Magus Tabor embodies precisely the metaphor of history as Gass presents it in this work. A magus was a priest-wiseman of ancient Persia, adept in the occult sciences of astrology and alchemy, who, as a consequence of his superior knowledge and abilities to do mysterious and wonderful things, was held in awe and feared by common people (as his students fear Magus Tabor). The word *magic* is rooted in this lore; therefore, the magus or magician in later times acquired its negativity, its association with sleight-of-hand and deception. The Magus is one of the Tarot cards, and has some of the same mystical properties that the planet Mercury (or its numen Hermes Trismegistus, mentioned by Tabor) has in astrology: ambivalence and intellectual rigor. John Fowles has made use of this symbol in his novel *The Magus,* and elsewhere in his writing.[16] Fowles's Conchis, a supposed Greek collaborator with the Nazis, inculcates (by means of an elaborate drama of initiation) in Nicholas, the protagonist, an awareness of the near-impossibility of knowing anything for certain. Facts never add up. Nicholas tries throughout the story to find out who Conchis is, what he really did in the war, and what he is doing to Nicholas in the present time of the story; in the end Conchis simply vanishes, leaving Nicholas to work out in his own life (or not) the precepts of the "drama." Gass's Magus, likewise, hypnotizes his students and visiting dignitaries through a manic performance on the lecture platform, saying in his own bizarre and twisted way the truth that historical fact is a "permanent unlikelihood." At the end of

his lecture, just before he disappears, he has his audience standing, antipho-
nally shouting GERMAN! GERMAN! GERMAN!: Magus Tabor then disappears. The audience takes to the streets to slake their hoarse throats at the
beer hall ("Mad Meg," 96).

What is the great and moving power inherent in this history or antihistory
lesson? To answer is to understand not only Gass's deepest worry about language and fiction but also the terrible seductiveness of the Nazi outrage.
Gass in this novel continues to issue warnings about the hazard of becoming
obsessed with language to the extent that a certain linguistic order takes the
place of the world, where moral vigor and right action are requisite. Gass sees
this potential replacement of the world by self-contained rhetorical systems as
an ineluctable possibility in art as well as in current affairs. The temptation to
consider history as a merely linguistic enterprise is dangerous: once the "ultimate ground" of reality is taken away, there are only "power plays" left. Gass
emphasizes that there is a reality that grounds and corrects doctrine. This
grounding negates the supposition that history is just a field of relativity between competing systems.[17]

Magus Tabor, nevertheless, goes against this grounding that Gass, broadly
summarizing Wittgenstein's public correction of private language,[18] says is
necessary to balance verbal systems that veer toward solipsism. Magus Tabor,
the wiley old preceptor whose words thunder and pound like a drumbeat (a
"tabor" is, after all, a drum), begins his "lecture" (actually a fusion in Kohler's
mind of a public lecture and private conversations with his teacher), his "ora-
tion" that in German tradition (and in early beerhall nazism) comes "before
beer," with the statement that historical inquiry does not really concern people, events, forces, movements, wars, and kingdoms ("Mad Meg," 86).
Tabor then goes into his antic theater of historical fact: he wrestles with these
"phantoms" (facts), hugging them to his chest, talking to them, denouncing
them as whores who give themselves to anyone, collecting them in an imaginary bucket like stones ("Mad Meg," 82). Kohler wonders why he and his
classmates did not laugh at such foolishness. Not one of them had the courage or the insight to label Tabor a clown. The listeners do not laugh because
there is something in them that longs for this kind of fiction, this kind of
drama, that satisfies their need to have the past put together in some seriously
artificial system, to have it "cobbled" for them, no matter how ridiculous or
insidious the fashion ("Mad Meg," 83).

As the audience sits hypnotized, Tabor drums away at his message that
history is an artifact made of words, like Gass's snowman, an artifact of snow-
balls, carrots, coals, buttons, and discarded clothing (a carrot "cobbled" into
the totality of the snowman loses its "particularity" to the mass). Language, in

other words, has preempted life: composition and history are inseparable, declares Tabor ("Mad Meg," 92). There is no such thing as *Wahrheit* (truth), insists Tabor, only competing texts of *Dichtung* (poetic, fictional composition). This is precisely Gass's definition of fascism: making a work of art out of real life—making things fit in to suit none but the needs of the artifact under construction.[19] Getting the work done regardless of how the materials must be stretched and bent is acceptable and indeed absolutely necessary for artwork; but art should not be mixed with the world; writing should be composed for itself and living as a responsible citizen should be done for itself. Irresponsible artistic pronouncements about life, particularly in the political sphere, are exceedingly dangerous; this belief is one of the major points that divide Gass's notions about writing from those of Gardner and other "realists."

If the Nazis created their crazed artifact, their evil Reich, out of convenient words, and if, as Tabor says, history is the study of words, fabrication of a weakly lived past ("Mad Meg," 94), then the present, as an extension of history, can be fabricated as well. If there is no truth to correct the word-machine, then there is a separate and perverted "literature" that real literature can have nothing to say to because the moral "ground" that Gass insists must be present is not there. There is no dialectical balance with such a monstrous work of art; even though it is captivating (Gass points out the seductiveness of anti-Semitism seen in this twisted way), and, as even great art is supposed to do, it replaces our consciousness with its own structure, it floats adrift in its own sea. Thus, the death camp commandant may leave that consciousness, just as he leaves the concert hall, go home to his family, and even read Goethe and Shakespeare, confident that he is involved in a necessary (dictated by the needs of the project) crusade (to create the purest, most perfectly cast object of beauty).

The serious historian, like Kohler and like all sincere interpreters of reality, is thus also a kind of fascist. He utilizes the carefully chosen data of the past to build a system for himself for whatever reason (to establish an academic reputation, to escape the guilt that Truth demeaned by Tabor attaches to all of us like lead weights). The key word here is *sincere*—serious, confident that one is engaged in a valuable, even heroic task and that the right thing (the longing of humankind) is to poetize and refashion time ("Mad Meg," 94).

If history, the recreation of time, is only a matter of the historian's dominion over words, then he who uses the words is he who grips the reins of rule in his hand. The world, says Tabor, was Greek or Roman because the literature, public documents, scientific statements, and the news were in Greek or Latin. Speech was at the core of conquest. Any historian who writes the history of another country in his own (i.e., different) language is "bent on conquest

("Mad Meg," 94–95). Eradicating other consciousnesses, rather than maintaining a dialectical relationship with them, accepting them as valid even if antithetical to our own, is for Gass the hallmark of fascism (*HW*, 239).

For Tabor, the "making of others," literally (as elements of the Artwork-State) and figuratively (as objects of sexual violation) is the logical next step in the process of historicizing the world. The thought and languages of other countries do not have the strength of those of the Germans, says the warped professor. Small countries like Albania and Belgium cannot write European history because their language and their vision cannot dominate, alter, or replace other languages, other folk traditions ("Mad Meg," 25). Take away Europe's tongue and you take away its consciousness; once its languages have been replaced by German, the path of domination is clear. Tabor shouts, beating cadence on the table, that the future will be German-speaking ("Mad Meg," 96).

This glorification of linguistic system, this transliteration of the pulses of reality into beautiful words, ignoring the grounding of truth, is what Mad Meg moves his teary-eyed Germans to adhere to and is what is immediately attractive to them: "going to his classes was like going to a circus or a carnival, a brothel even; certain standards were suspended for the visit" ("Mad Meg," 94). Meg's words seduce so effectively because, like art and music, they are a world all their own, a separate life that can be entered and left like Babs Masters's bed. There is no carryover from the realm of words to the domain of responsible action; there is no lasting conditioning of the moral self. Therefore, as Gass says repeatedly, fictions (word systems) have no ultimate pedagogical impact on morals. Like a ferocious animal behind bars at a zoo, Meg is confined like a specimen in his lecture ("Mad Meg," 94). His obvious, immediate danger has been removed; his metaphorical unreality (artificiality) is the precise vehicle that allows his words to reach his students and other listeners ("Mad Meg," 94). Tabor, kept within the confines of his lecture hall and taken for what he really is, an illusionist, a magician, an entertainer, is harmless. It is only when he is taken seriously, let out into the streets, into politics, that he is no longer beautiful.

Kohler sees Tabor for what he is, "not a dangerous explosive as he [Meg] liked to hint" but as a "fuse" (94). Hitler was a clownish word-twister, an eccentric exhibitionist, until his words were taken to heart, allowed to create for the German people a viable fiction without the benefit of correction by the truth. Kohler, however, persists in writing, and thereby twisting, history as though it had objective force. His motive is power, linguistic power to exonerate himself from having thrown a brick at a Jew's window, becoming, even as merely an American of German lineage, a colleague of the Nazis. The the-

sis of his book, that there was perhaps an innocence, his innocence, to coun-
terbalance the terrible guilt that the mass suppression of truth had built up in
a nation, is fake. He knows Tabor's tricks; he knows the culpability of the
Nazis. Yet he keeps on tunnelling and writing his preface, trying desperately
to put his lies to rest so that his book can take the place of what really happened. He is a prisoner of his book, and, as his wife says, he will never be able
to live outside it. Like Gass in writing "The Tunnel," Kohler can never reach
closure with his preface, can never reconcile his life with *Guilt and Innocence
in Hitler's Germany.*

Kohler experiences tremendous difficulty dealing with his guilt because he
seeks a verbal, an academic solution to his own Jewish question, his own
shame; he tries to reduce his culpability by pretending that his scholarly language has rendered the past as it was. Kohler, in his hermeneutic, linguistic
attempt at self-exculpation, is constantly reminded, nevertheless, of his guilt
by Culp. Culp (from the Latin, *culpa,* guilt) spends his time composing a history of the world entirely in limericks. Kohler is as haunted by the phantom
of Culp as he is by the memory of Tabor. Even when Kohler is not physically
interacting with Culp and his other colleagues at the university, he is engaged
in a running dialogue with him in his mind. Kohler hates Culp's limerick history because it is a sarcastic counterpart to Kohler's own serious book; Culp's
humorous playfulness is an indictment of Kohler's vain attempt to see
history/fiction as more than what it really is, just words. Culp's work, in
other words, is a healthy counterweight to Kohler's in that it constantly
points to itself as something made up, something not to be confused with real
life. Kohler, between verses of Culp's limericks, plots to himself the imaginary (or is it the actual?) death of the latter. Perhaps he will use a ray gun, or a
death-camp oven ("Windows," 290–91).

Culp's ability to laugh at the story of the human race hacks at Kohler's
delicate defense of his belief in history as a refuge, a way of exerting power
over his life, and an exculpation for past actions. Other peers with whom he
carries on extended arguments and who irritate him as much as Culp represent less confrontational notions about the nature of time and human events.
Herschel, the Cartesian of the group, always begins with his own version of
Descartes's *cogito:* "I sometimes think" ("Windows," 290). Kohler wonders
whether Herschel can think at all in his milquetoast, self-effaced manner,
afraid to confront the world ("Windows," 290). And even though Herschel
holds the opinion that history will parallel the development of human consciousness into self-reflexivity, thereby coming close enough to Kohler's
views to become Kohler's "muse," he is too meek to force his own artificial
persona on the world; he is "nebbish . . . one one kicks" ("Windows," 290).

Disagreeing with any such attempt to find meaning in evidence from the past, Oscar Planmantee, another of these troublesome fellow academics, brushes off "mankind like a piece of lint."[20] Oscar, Kohler's "nemesis," considers events like things, able to be broken down like pieces of bread into some basic, atomistic reality ("Old Folks," 36). Kohler, while spending sizable amounts of his time debating with his department peers, in the end cannot agree with any of them; their views, although contradictory and fractured, are for him basically the same. Time for each is linear ("Old Folks," 36).

This conclave of professors with their insistence that history has some content or some purpose only reinforces Kohler's inability to put an end to his own history; his fellow scholars, with their discordant theories and biases, make Kohler ask himself if human consciousness, the matter of history, is only a poison kingdom of dreams, a senseless agglutination of events[21] that has no sense to it, only an ignominious end ("Susu," 137). Kohler's tunnel, the one "really" dug in his basement as well as the imaginary burrowing through life that takes place in his chair, in his writing and rewriting of events in time, leads nowhere, even though there is the hope of a possible escape. There is no light at the end of Kohler's tunnel.

"Causes beyond Guilt"

Kohler's tunneling is an attempt to bury himself and any possible readers in his arrangement of data that of necessity have accrued from his vain attempt to burrow into the past of Nazi Germany, a past that is cemented around his own, a past that he must vainly try to leave behind: "When I write about the Third Reich, or now, when I write about myself, is it the truth I want? What DO I want? We drag our acts behind us like a string of monsters."[22] Kohler's personal history contains the seeds of the Holocaust; Kohler, in his very being, is a fascist. His participation in *Kristallnacht,* his casting of the brick at a Jew's window, is a violation that he himself feels deeply owing to his reverence for windows as a meeting ground of the mind and whatever is meant by reality beyond the glass. The brick throwing returns to pollute his thoughts and his dreams, and is in large part the principal event of his history, both in the book (public) and in his preface (private). As he remembers bringing his children to visit his parents for the first time, his mind fastens upon a smaller act of violence from his childhood: the original breaking of windows to be replicated in his vile act on *Kristallnacht.* As a child he had shot beebees into the windows of a neighbor's house. Forty years

later, he remembers this incident because he cannot forget the "shit that followed," his punishment from his father ("Old Folks," 41).

Kohler's statement that he remembers "the shit that followed" summarizes "The Tunnel"; it is the very definition of history with which he struggles.
The remembrance of past actions and their consequences is the principal element of history and the element that haunts Kohler. The relationship between the beebee shot through the window and the brick tossed on
Kristallnacht, the kinship of the child Kohler to his older self (the "shit that
followed," despite the "grandeur" that Gass seeks to give him), directs the
narrative force of the novel as it does the path of the narrator's thoughts. If
Kohler's *Guilt and Innocence in Hitler's Germany* "gentles" the ultimate brutality of the Holocaust, his personal history inscribed in its far-wandering
preface is a vain effort to ameliorate the inherent evil in his personality. He
deceives himself that the present-day Kohler is a new creature. He can now
speak gently to himself, he thinks.[23]

This gentle speaking is a melodic essay on time and its effects on the mind.
In this part, Kohler has escaped from the quotidian, from his daily routines
and obligations as husband, father, professor, and writer of history books.
"Pleading the pressures of work" ("Summer Bees," 231), he has run away
with Lou, one of his lovers, for an extramarital romp in an upstairs room in
the country. This is the most strenuous of Kohler's drives to separate himself
from his past. His persona presents itself as a series of splits or syzygies. He
seeks out all that appears the opposite of what he is. Lou at first glance is not
at all like Martha, his wife. Martha, "a master of genealogical botany,"[24]
never gives her preoccupation with her family history a rest, never forgets the
importance of "lineal derivations" and "connections" ("Cost"). Lou, like
Kohler's other two lovers, Rue and Susu (the rhyming triad of female pres-
ences about whose reality one is never quite sure), is rootless, rebellious, and
has no sympathy for history. Lou insists that a picture of a Civil War encampment that hangs on the wall of their room in western New York be turned
around. Removing the collected public memories that the historical photograph symbolizes allows for a moment out of time, a paradise that permits
Lou to fulfill her desire of having "all of me [Kohler]" ("Summer Bees," 233)
and Kohler to live without time: "And didn't we have a clock we kept in the
pocket of its case—somewhere a quiet tick, a measure we forgot?" ("Summer
Bees," 232).

This Edenic bliss, out of time and off the record of history, acquires in
Kohler's telling a descriptive intensity that enhances its dreaminess. They go
for walks and swim and read and take loose-limbed naps in the afternoon
("Summer Bees," 232–33). Kohler, writing the twelfth chapter of his book, a

chapter about children, about the Nazi perversion of the German school system, composes with ease, thoughtlessly ("Summer Bees," 233). Like Adam,
Kohler revels in the act of standing nude, feeling the brush of a breeze against
the hair of his legs like the caress of Lou's breath before the pressure of her
tongue on his skin ("Summer Bees," 233). The summer place and time stand
in contrast to the "winter room" the couple had shared, a room filled with the
"snow" that had fallen between them and the cold wind blown on them by
the thoughts of Kohler's married status. The summer residence contains no
ties to profession, family, or the world outside ("Summer Bees," 233). Although Kohler can delight in his momentary escape from the quotidian and
be content in this ritual absence from history, Lou wants the moment to last.
She cannot deal with a man who is stuck in the middle of a tunnel. She wants
a final solution, a swift passage through the tunnel into her territory; she has
no patience with "EINE, MEINE, MINE, MU" ("Summer Bees," 233).

Lou, like Omensetter and Kick's cat, beckons to Kohler to lose himself totally in somatic carelessness. Lou is one of those beings whose minds seem
buried in flesh, "whose souls are the same as their skins," and therefore who,
mortally afraid of the unredeemable physical decomposition brought on by
time, want desperately to be nothing but what they already have been—
unchanged ("Summer Bees," 234). Lou (from the French, *lieu,* place) *is* a
place: her "twat" is "an enchanted forest," a "furry tunnel" ("Summer Bees,"
234–35). While Lou can make Kohler stop midway in (his) her tunnel for a
rest, breathe in vapors from the Garden of Innocence, she cannot crawl along
with him forever in mindless irresponsibility. She must stay *in her place,* stay
the way she is. Like Odysseus, Kohler is fated to leave Kalypso (oblivion, paradise), to continue tunneling with no real end in sight. Embedded in his
words of joyful thanks for his brief moment of happiness with Lou are other
words that make that happiness seem ephemeral. Kohler's historically
trained mind can look to the end of his life, a life ultimately destroyed by
time, and attempt to find some solace, and—if not consolation—at least a
modicum of authenticity (a very loose paraphrase of Heidegger's temporali-
zation of time), in knowing that people change, even if the change is toward
death. His mind can stand outside itself and, looking to the end of his existence, extract itself from the prison of daily life that seeks to suggest change-
lessness. This possibility of change presents the opportunity for a redemption
of sorts: a "shit" acquires "grandeur."

The possibility of escape from history, a time-out from the attempt to render the past in language, is illusory. Language, as well as one of its principal
products, history, is condemned to flicker between the border of its own self-
absorbed structure and that of its connection with the world. The beautiful

restfulness of Kohler's summer with Lou is brought into focus painfully by means of the symbolic stinging of the bees. Kohler's perfect summer world with Lou is doomed to disappear. Summer, a time of life and vitality, must ultimately yield to autumn and the return to the still deathliness of winter. Within the fullness of the vernal there is the emptiness of the hibernal. The bee, symbolic of busy activity and floral life, possesses a stinger. Although the picture of the Civil War encampment is turned to the wall, its image persists relentlessly in Kohler's mind. He cannot really escape his professional life; there is always the back of the picture (which is described as carefully as the front) as there is winter (the other side of summer) and the anger of Lou (brought on by the pain in her bee-stung breasts) to balance the infantile rest from cares symbolized by the happy, beautifully breasted Lou (the summer place, *lieu*). Again, as in all of Gass's metaphorical narrative structures, the author stresses the concept of syzygy: the fullness of one element of reality carries within it the kernel of its opposite. The surfacing of the syzygy is the movement not only of narrative but of history as well.

In the summer Eden with Lou, Kohler can write almost automatically his chapter on the Nazi indoctrination of German children. The seeming lack of concern and fluidity in this part of Kohler's writing matches the childlike simplicity of Kohler's Shangri-la with Lou. The manner of writing also parallels the content. The romantic notion that children, if taught a new way of thinking, can become a generation of robots who conform to the ideals of adults is the topic of Kohler's chapter. It is also the matter symbolized by Lou: that mankind can return to a state of perfection, liberated from the shackles (cares, vices, inhibitions, fears, myths, traditions) of the past. All educational systems, especially those that hope for a revolutionary return to innocence and the domination of (through liberation from) the past, attempt to redirect childhood, the supposed tabula rasa of humanity. But youth, as a clean slate, does not exist; for, in the garden of childhood, lives the serpent of the adult. The young Kohler with his beebee gun trained on a neighbor's window inexorably turns into the adult Kohler with a brick in his hand on *Kristallnacht,* and in later life turns again into the Kohler who, although having learned to respect the truth and sanctity of windows, tries nevertheless to penetrate the glass in which all things "swim," to penetrate the absent past. The story of Lou is thus a reiteration of the familiar Gass lesson of the Garden: childhood (innocence) is a fabrication of the mind. Those majestic "summer bees" in the paradise of our imaginations, when translated to reality, deliver painful stings.

If Lou personifies a locus of unthinking, childlike peace in Kohler's mind, Susu represents the contrary and evil nature of his youth, and youth in general. Tied to Kohler's fallen, self-aware state, Susu is an amalgam of Mad Meg (Kohler states that Susu might well be Meg ["Susu," 122]), Kohler's parents, Kohler as a professor, and Kohler's relationship with nazism in general. Susu emblemizes the mentality of a fascist: she is "a slime of green down a wet wall ("Susu," 122). This repulsive metaphor leads to many others in the image-cluster that produces this character. The first, the metaphorical core of the story "Susu I Approach You in My Dreams," is that of a Gypsy thumbsucker, the juxtaposition of an insecure childhood and a young life spent moving constantly from one place to another. This is a reflection of Kohler's life with his parents during the depression and also of the life of the children in post–World War I Germany who grew up to fill Hitler's legions. The name *Susu* stresses the syllabic replication that young children make in their prelanguage development ("mama," "dada," and so forth). Susu, although degenerate and vile, is fundamentally a child; she seems to have no will, no hardness of substance; she is small and frail; she is described as sucking a thumb. The familiar fact of childish thumbsucking, however, is drawn into a monstrous figural extension: the thumbs that Susu sucks are the thumbs of Jews killed by the Nazis. Such an outlandish perversion (either in Kohler's imagination or in reality) mocks the Nazi idealization (corruption) of youth that is the subject of Kohler's chapter on the German schools. Susu, the slender Gypsy cabaret singer, becomes, either willingly out of *abulia,* or out of fear, a whore of the Nazis; she is "used," "admired," "loved," and ultimately decapitated by them ("Susu," 123). She is ruined, as were most young Germans, by her association with institutionalized evil. Her portrait, the image held always before us, is that of a "lustful," "passive" fiend who gnaws on the dead ("Susu," 135). Her participation in the atrocities, even if only symbolic and indirect, focuses her forever in history (in the mind of one historian, at least) as a "little" person, a microentity in the larger field, but one inextricably welded to the darkest and the most brutal. She is damned by her destiny (her nature and circumstances).

Kohler's hurling of a brick, an act of youthful irresponsibility, a magnification of shooting beebees at windows, likewise cannot be forgiven. Although neither the brick nor the beebees caused serious physical damage, the mentality that produced Kohler's acts was responsible for millions of deaths. Kohler writes, with the repetitiveness of a refrain, that even though he is an expert on Nazi Germany, he never "[goes] there" ("Susu," 132); however, the truth is the contrary: he can never really leave the Nazi Germany of his thoughtless student days because of this guilt. He is, like Susu "in his dreams," inherently (uncontrollably), by "destiny" a Nazi ("Susu," 122).

Another dimension of the Susu image grows out of her association with the many houses that the Kohler family occupied throughout Billy's childhood. Kohler (like Gass himself) describes his childhood as floating, Moses-like, in a basket from his birthplace along the rivers of northeastern Ohio, particularly the Mahoning, a river as dirty as Susu ("a slit-open eel on a dirty plate" ["Susu," 123]). Susu, called "filth" by Kohler, attaches herself like a leech to the Kohler-Moses (Moses as the prototype of the Wandering Jew) image, turning it sour. She is the dark side of wandering; as such, her identification in Kohler's mind with the many bathrooms the Kohler family occupied as a result of constant moving from house to house is understandable. Susu, in the same sentence dedicated to a description of the senior Kohler's bathroom painting (he painted each bathroom, the dirtiest part of each house, in bright enamel), is characterized as "singing out of earshot" and attempting to see herself in "empty mirrors" ("Susu," 124). Singing to oneself and looking at oneself in medicine cabinet mirrors are popular bathroom activities. A magnified image of Susu in this regard embodies the towns and rivers of Kohler's youth. Like toilets connected to a common sewer, the small industrial cities on the river that Billy Kohler grew up in were dominated by the pollution disgorged by "yellow-tasting cloud machines" ("Susu," 124) where windows (dear to Kohler even then) were "grime glazed" ("Susu," 125).

Billy Kohler, himself a rootless, dirty little Gypsy, recalls the even poorer sections of these towns ("open zoos of the ghettos" ["Susu," 125]) the way he saw them through the windows of the family car as he and his parents drove through, with him singing "hit songs" (Susu-like) in the security of the back seat ("Susu," 125). His recollections are couched in words of racism and violence: he remembers "coons" with "nigger-eyes" like the white globes boys shot out with beebee guns (another tentacle extending from the window-breaking metaphor), and striking workers ("wops," "Polacks," "Bohunks," "micks," and "kike"-hating "heinies") beating at scabs and police with sticks ("Susu," 125). He assigns these people to their appointed workstations: Greeks in their restaurants, Italians in crime and groceries, Jews in lowly finance, Poles at the furnaces, blacks at their push brooms ("Susu," 125). These "little people" that Herschel advises Kohler to include in the blame for nazism are better left on the other side of the glass, "enameled over," flushed from memory. They are not really (in their raw form) the prime material of history in Kohler's view—they are the milieu in which Kohler actually would like to make himself invisible, "like the Marquis de Sade or, like Susu" ("Susu," 127), the camp out of which he would like to escape by tunnel, "spilling ink" ("Susu," 141).

Such people are certainly not exempt from blame for evil, but neither are

they clearly to blame. Sophisticated people are just as guilty, and by extension, just as innocent. Nazis recruit from all levels of society; atrocities, therefore, arise from the ignorance and blind allegiance of "little people" as well as
the back turning of the enlightened (conductors of orchestras, professors,
lawyers, industrialists, clergy, those who—to continue the toilet image—
"moved their bowels daily in homage to the Greeks" ["Susu," 128–29]). All
people, rich and poor, "big" and "little," powerful and powerless, and especially women (in general), deserve, in Kohler's mind, the blame for Hitler or
any other vicious perversion. Real heroes and villains exist nowhere but in
storybooks ("Susu," 131). The reality of history is that people are both good
and evil with intense simultaneity.

Tunneling "out," therefore, is impossible; there are no "genuine Germans" to get away from. To seek such people would be like identifying
one's own father—even if he is a bit of a "household kaiser," as Kohler Senior seemed to Billy—as a "filthy hun" ("Susu," 141). Although there
would be a small truth in it, this is obviously absurd. Kohler's true feelings
about his father are almost impossible to express, as he discovers when he
tries to dedicate his book to his father and ends up erasing the intended
dedication. Even Magus Tabor and Susu deserve no ultimate censure for
nazism; the only "final solution" to anything is the obliteration of all
problems—the erasure of human life itself ("Susu," 141). This is a wise insight for a fascist; we can applaud the "grandeur" of a well-stated concept,
even if it comes from someone like Kohler.

Susu, therefore, in her cruelty, her insensitivity, her lack of substance, both
exists and does not really exist for Kohler. Her singing and her fear of death
link her closely to the imaginary self of Kohler. The latter can never actually
become a mindless, diabolical Susu anymore than he can arrive at a place in
time congruent with Lou (*lieu*), or gain a position in Paradise. He cannot find
escape in perfection nor can he find it in flaw. He can only "approach being"
Susu just as he can possess Lou only in his dreams. Susu and Lou, as they lin-
ger in Kohler's mind, merely empty forms and "wraiths," are both likely to
vanish at any moment ("Susu," 135), leaving only Kohler in his chair to perpetuate their names and their essences within himself (as Billy's father will
die, leaving only the feel of the shaking he gave his son and as the son will in
turn unjustly shake his own son). Susu and Lou are both symbolic out-
growths of Kohler's puerile nature, a preordained core present even in his
tender childhood and around which the Kohler who is now fifty has developed the layers of his being.

Ruth (Rue)

The entity identified by the name Ruth is multilayered and dialectical with regard to other such metaphors (characters). One of the levels of the symbolism of Ruth comes directly from the Old Testament, from the book of the same name.[25] It is the story of a girl, already a widow, who marries a much older man. This situation fits perfectly with the relationship between Kohler and his young female students, in particular with one named Ruth. The story is also appropriate because it has to do with leaving behind parents and a way of life and going to live among strangers: this relates directly to Kohler's youth at home and in Germany.

Like the biblical Ruth, Kohler's Ruth (Rue) has turned her back on her parents, having (unlike Kohler's wife) no "head for lineal derivations" ("Cost"). She seems very young, childlike, "plays gipsy baby" ("Cost"). She is in a subservient position to an older man (pupil to teacher, one of Kohler's "slaves") with whom she has an oral sexual relationship. Like her ancient counterpart, Rue is childishly obedient: "Just tell me what you want me to, and I'll do it" ("Cost"). Kohler bribes Rue with ice cream; it is the "rising cost" of having student love slaves. Rue, who lives on milk, suffers not from adult diseases like "gout, stone, or consumption," but from the "colic of an infant" ("Cost"). Rue has hands like a baby, unpracticed fingers that play with Kohler's penis as though she has had no prior experience in such matters. Juxtaposed to Kohler's recollection of Rue's baby hands is the memory of his mother's hands and her polished nails, hands that possessed the "carelessness of a shitting bird" ("Cost"). Like those of an infant, the hands of little Rue can fit entirely in her mouth; this mouth–hand relationship calls to Kohler's mind the breasts of his wife, Martha, when she was young, breasts small enough to fit entirely into his mouth one at a time. This is another tying-in to the central composite image of "the female" in Kohler's life: his wife, his student sexual adventure, and his mother. This character–plot unit suggests many significant polarities. The first is intertextual—the link between the Bible and Kohler's preface ("The Tunnel"), both commentaries on historical periods—the era of the Judges in Israel and the Nazi outrage. The texts thus also emphasize the tragic dual vision of Kohler as he writes and thinks constantly about the "Jewish Problem."

The name Ruth highlights the complexity of the biblical treatment of place (home, tribe, race), the sacred and the profane, the sedentary versus the moving life, parents estranged from children, age in conflict with youth, and Kohler's attempt to deal with those same elements of his own life. Ruth, the Moabitess, who has rejected her lineage to join herself to the seed of the most eminent family of all time, is contrasted with Rue the babyish student who both rejects her family and hates the seed of Kohler (a would-be Boaz) on her hands, although she is not averse to mud ("Cost"). She disrespectfully catches his semen in a paper cup and, like a silly child, watches it turn brown as time passes.

Kohler's wife, Martha, is placed in diametrical tension with both Rue and Ruth of Moab. Like Rue, she accepts Kohler's seed in her mouth; but unlike the infantile student, the wife has great respect for her place in the family line, her own as well as that which she and Kohler establish. She bears the fruit of that seed that Rue mocks. She is no longer a plaything; her breasts no longer fit in Kohler's mouth because she has grown older; like her New Testament (Luke 10:38–42) namesake, she bears the responsibility of the house. A mother, an aging woman, her breasts have swelled along with her cares.

Kohler's mother, the most important component of this triangle, makes a medial opposition with both Rue and Martha: her age counters and thereby emphasizes the youth of Rue and her impending death gnaws at Kohler's mind, reminding him that the life that parents give to children is subtracted from their own; as children grow, parents wane. Kohler is painfully aware that he is now "old folks" ("Old Folks," 46).

The polarity of youth and old age fixed by the Ruth metaphor makes up the heart of the novel. The name *Ruth,* calling to mind an old story laden with preestablished meaning, also has meaning in itself. The Hebrew word translates as "companion," while the noncognate archaic English means "guilt, regret." The "ruth" about the loss of youth, of time's passage, which is the real current of history, is an unshakable "companion" for Kohler. History is not a series of events like "things" that can be analyzed (broken "like bread" into parts) and synthesized (parts reconstituted as an "ultimate element" or "changeless penny" ["Old Folks," 136]). History is dual, both happy and diabolical, with no middle; guilt and innocence mingle like two rivers flowing simultaneously in the same bed. History is nothing but the birth and death of humanity: "human coupling, human pain" ("Old Folks," 37). Even as a child, Kohler felt history as really only a matter of entropy: "the sweet world of wish and rich invention" that always came to an end "as every holiday does, and ending emptily pushed out like the last stool" ("Life in a Chair," 35).

Although Kohler functions as an "accountant" accumulating and analyzing trivia, for the most part, all his attempts to catch and keep life (putting the bloody X on his parents and his hometown to keep away the Angel of Death ["Old Folks," 35]) are in vain. Kohler achieves a steady vision of time, a cause in history apart from guilt, apart from innocence. Lou, Susu, and Rue, like rhyming magnets, all draw out this truth about time, allowing

Kohler (in his dialectical relationship with this trio of alter selves) to demonstrate his substantial wisdom about human life from childhood to old age, a wisdom uncommon in a Fascist "shit," even a "shit" shot through with "grandeur." Passage through time's tunnel must leave debris—and that is all that is left, despite attempts at beautification through historiography.

If, as Gass has said, "The Tunnel" is a "turning back to inspect directly" the debris of his childhood, then we can envision in this yet-to-be-released novel a paradigm of postmodern writing: a writer writing about a writer in a chair writing to "cancel the consequences of the past."[26]

Afterword

The fiction of William Gass is a literature of tension and symmetrical opposition. His narrative grows out of a slow and tedious system of writing and rewriting sentences, each series of images balancing others and promoting the gradual emergence of a gracefully extended metaphor. Often there are moments of meaning that reach a profound assessment of the human condition. These points of intense revelation develop as a result of the struggle of opposing forces, bipolar elements of a field of resonance that has kept Gass's writing at the leading edge of contemporary serious fiction.

Like Pynchon's Oedipa, who is both unsure of the existence of Tristero, the system that calls to her, and at the same time imagines herself becoming part of it,[1] Gass's isolated narrators—Furber, Tott, Jorge Pedersen, the poet in "B . . ."—all seek refuge from the reality of the daily life around them and at the same time try somehow to escape from solipsism, reaching out (unsuccessfully) to close with human society and love. Sets of characters, like those in "Icicles," bring to Gass's work an allegorical dimension; this is, according to Brian McHale, "a characteristic mode of postmodernist writing."[2] These pairings of characters, armatures for the embodiment of symbols, produce the constant interplay of dualities like nature and culture in *Omensetter's Luck*, childhood and adult society in "The Pedersen Kid," daily life and eternity in "Order of Insects," motherhood and female sexuality in "Mrs. Mean," the book and the reader in *Willie Masters' Lonesome Wife*. Out of these bipolar oppositions come the whirling wheels of Gass's metaphor, spinning emblems that supplant in the reader's mind the overworked notion of linearity in fiction. Deftly shaped imagery is bolstered by a driving metrical pulse; musicality reinforces the dense language in William Gass, drawing readers into the superbly assembled webs of words that loop constantly around themselves, drawing the mind away from the world and into what Saltzman calls the "consolation of language."

Not only do these points of dialectic emphasize an allegory of polarity after the fashion of Ishmael Reed (*Mumbo Jumbo*), Robert Coover (*The Public Burning*), and John Barth (*Giles Goatboy*), but they also place Gass in a school of contemporary American fiction writers whose experimentalism appears to have grown into a lasting body of literature: what Wilde and others have labeled the "midfictionists," or mature modernists. Writers like Gass,

Coover, Pynchon, Reed, Elkin, Apple, and Barthelme have battled conventional fiction's fixation on representation but at the same time have avoided becoming lost in the blizzard of language. These writers have joined with Joyce, Faulkner, and the other great modernists to produce a fiction that resonates between the beautiful illusions of words and the nagging realities of the objective world.

This middle stance has not come easy for William Gass. He has since childhood been in angry confrontation with many extreme aspects of his environment. He has even worked against himself, against his own theoretical system, in order to test the limits of a prose that points always to the most basic of human desires, to the need for love, acceptance, but also to the requirements of playfulness, honesty, and dignity.

Notes and References

Preface

1. I use this term in the way that Alan Wilde uses it, although he excludes Gass (but not Elkin) from what he calls "midfictionists." See his *Middle Grounds: Studies in Contemporary American Fiction* (Philadelphia: University of Pennsylvania Press, 1987).

2. Again, I express my debt to the thesis of Wilde's *Middle Grounds*, particularly as expressed in his first forty pages.

Chapter One

1. Quoted from "A Colloquium with William H. Gass and Brooke K. Horvath, Ruth H. Porritt, Martin P. Rapisarda, Carol F. Richer: William T. Stafford, Moderator," *Modern Fiction Studies* 4, no. 29 (Winter 1983): 591.

2. Larry McCaffery, "The Gass-Gardner Debate: Showdown on Mainstreet," *Literary Review* 23, no. 1 (Fall 1979): 134–44.

3. John Gardner, quoted in Thomas LeClair, *Anything Can Happen: Interviews with Contemporary American Novelists* (Urbana: University of Illinois Press, 1983), 23.

4. LeClair, *Anything Can Happen*, 22.

5. Ibid.

6. Larry McCaffery, *The Metafictional Muse: The Works of Robert Coover, Donald Barthelme, and William H. Gass* (Pittsburgh: University of Pittsburgh Press, 1982), 256.

7. Quoted in "Colloquium with William H. Gass," 597.

8. See John Barth's "The Literature of Exhaustion," in *Surfiction: Fiction Now . . . and Tomorrow*, ed. Raymond Federman (Chicago: Swallow Press, 1975), 19–33.

9. I wish to express here my debt to the first chapter of McCaffery's *Metafictional Muse*.

10. See Alain Robbe-Grillet, *For a New Novel: Essays on Fiction*, trans. Richard Howard (New York: Grove Press, 1965), 10–11.

11. McCaffery, *Metafictional Muse*, 4.

12. LeClair, *Anything Can Happen*, 155.

13. See Robert Sanford's interview with Gass in the *St. Louis Post-Dispatch*, 3 June 1973, 2G.

14. "William H. Gass," in *World Authors: 1950–1970*, ed. John Wakeman, (New York: H. W. Wilson, 1975), 537.

15. LeClair, *Anything Can Happen*, 154–55.

16. Quoted in *World Authors*, 537.

17. Ibid.

18. Quoted in *World Authors*, 538.

19. Ibid.

20. LeClair, *Anything Can Happen*, 155.

21. "Colloquy with William H. Gass," 597.

22. Ibid.

23. Ibid.

24. Ibid.

25. *In the Heart of the Heart of the Country* appears in the second volume of the 1987 edition of *The Harper American Literature* (New York: Harper & Row). *Forms of Literature* (New York: Random House, 1989) features essays on literature written by students; two of these essays cite William Gass.

26. Larry McCaffery, "William Gass," in *Dictionary of Literary Biography* (Detroit: Gale Research Company, 1979), 190.

27. LeClair, *Anything Can Happen*, 157.

28. "William H. Gass," in *World Authors 1950–1970*, 538.

29. LeClair, *Anything Can Happen*, 152.

30. Ibid., 153.

31. Ibid., 163.

32. McCaffery, "William Gass," *Dictionary of Literary Biography*, 191.

33. Quoted by Carole Spearin McCauley in *The New Fiction: Interviews with Innovative American Writers*, ed. Joe David Bellamy (Urbana: University of Illinois Press, 1974), 42.

34. Richard Gilman, review of *Omensetter's Luck, New Republic,* 7 May 1966, 23.

35. Review of *Omensetter's Luck, Newsweek,* 18 April 1966, 114.

36. The title for this section is quoted from Gass's *Fiction and the Figures of Life* (New York: Alfred A. Knopf, 1970), 118; hereafter cited as *FFL* in the text.

37. Don Crinklaw, "It's All a Matter of Style" (interview), *St. Louis Post-Dispatch,* 5 March 1972, 4C.

38. McCaffery, *Metafictional Muse,* 6.

39. Ibid.

40. Raymond Federman, *Surfiction: Fiction Now . . . and Tomorrow* (Chicago: Swallow Press), 11

41. Bellamy, *The New Fiction,* 56.

42. "A Symposium on Fiction (Barthelme, Gass, Paley, Percy)," *Shenandoah* 27 (Winter 1976): 8.

43. Bellamy, *The New Fiction,* 35.

44. Ibid.

45. "A Symposium," 8.

46. The subtitle for this section is quoted from LeClair, *Anything Can Happen*, 163.

47. John Barth, "The Literature of Replenishment," *Atlantic Monthly*, June 1980, 66. Brian McHale, in his refreshingly clear study of postmodernism, *Postmodernist Fiction* (New York: Methuen, 1987), quotes this same Barth statement (p. 3). I wish to express my appreciation of and debt to McHale's fine book.

48. Charles Newman, "The Post-Modern Aura: The Act of Fiction in an Age of Inflation," quoted in McHale, *Postmodernist Fiction*, 3.

49. Ibid.

50. Ibid., 9.

51. Ibid., 7–10

52. Ibid., 10

53. Ibid.

54. LeClair, *Anything Can Happen*, 167.

55. Arthur M. Saltzman, *The Fiction of William Gass: The Consolation of Language* (Carbondale and Edwardsville: Southern Illinois Press, 1986).

56. Saltzman, *Fiction of William Gass*, 170.

57. LeClair, *Anything Can Happen*, 169.

58. Ibid.

59. McCauley in *The New Fiction*, 42.

60. LeClair, *Anything Can Happen*, 25.

61. Ibid., 26.

62. Ibid., 25.

63. Ibid., 170.

64. Ibid.

65. Ibid.

66. McHale, *Postmodernist Fiction*, 140. See Maureen Quilligan, *The Language of Allegory: Defining the Genre* (Ithaca, N.Y.: Cornell University Press, 1979), 155.

67. Quilligan, *Language of Allegory*, 155.

68. Ibid.

69. McHale, *Postmodernist Fiction*, 144.

70. I refer to the comments of Denis Donoghue in his *Ferocious Alphabets* (Boston: Little, Brown, 1981), 89.

71. LeClair, *Anything Can Happen*, 30.

Chapter Two

1. See David Jones, *Epoch and Artist* (London: Faber & Faber, 1959), 123–25.

2. See Gass's discussion of symbolist theoretician Paul Valéry, in *WWW* 158–76, and Saltzman's consideration of Furber as representative of the symbolists' dream of the linguistic reification of Edenic perfection, in *Fiction of William Gass*, 43.

3. Jeffrey L. Duncan, "A Conversation with Stanley Elkin and William H.

Gass," *Iowa Review* 7 (Winter 1976): 60. In the interview with Don Crinklaw of the *St. Louis Post-Dispatch* (3 June 1973), Gass stated that his work has been influenced by Bach, Bartók, and Schoenberg (as well as a good many other polysymphonic composers). "That kind of influence is a sense of visible structure," he said. "My sense of a work's form is musical: 'modulation,' 'theme and variations.'" See Joseph Chiari, *Symbolisme from Poe to Mallarmé: The Growth of a Myth* (New York: Gordian Press, 1970), 44–45, for a clear discussion of the interest in music among the *Symbolistes.*

4. *The World within the Word* (New York: Alfred A. Knopf, 1978), 330; hereafter cited in the text as *WWW.*

5. *Habitations of the Word* (New York: Simon & Schuster, 1985), 178; hereafter cited in the text as *HW.*

6. Omensetter's Luck (New York: New American Library, 1966), 89; hereafter cited in the text.

7. Duncan Emrich, *Folklore of the American Land* (Boston: Little, Brown, 1972), 285.

8. Robert A. Georges, "The General Concept of Legend," in *American Folk Legend: A Symposium,* ed. Wayland Hand (Berkeley and Los Angeles: University of California Press, 1971), 12–13.

9. Ibid.

10. Yoder's essay also appears in *American Folk Legend: A Symposium,* ed. 157–83.

11. Yoder, *American Folk Legend,* 160, writes: "From the use of the saints, angels, archangels, Mary, and the Trinity in the world of the folk-medical incantations and charms, one gets a reminiscence, in Pennsylvania, across the Atlantic, and four centuries after the Reformation, of the medieval *Weltbild* of the heavenly hierarchies so frequently portrayed in Catholic art—academic, popular, and folk."

12. I wish to express my debt to B. A. Botkin's classic collection of folk literature, *A Treasury of American Folklore* (New York: Crown Publishers, 1944), especially pages 768–918.

13. Botkin, *A Treasury of American Folklore,* 771.

14. Emrich, *Folklore on the American Land* (Boston: Little, Brown, 1972), 257.

15. M. L. von Franz, *Man and His Symbols* (New York: Doubleday/Windfall, 1983), 208.

16. C. G. Jung, *Aion,* in *Collected Works,* vol. 9, pt. 2 (Princeton, N.J.: Princeton University Press, 1959), 170.

17. I have made use of Jung's *Aion,* particularly the chapter "The Ambivalence of the Fish Symbol," for this brief summary of the symbolic nature of the fish. This subject is overwhelming; consequently, summarizing is difficult.

18. Jung, *Aion,* 125.

19. Jung, *Aion,* 119, cites the Midrash Tanchuma and a poem by Meir ben Isaac.

20. Gass confessed to lack of ability at "straight narrative" in an interview with Don Crinklaw in the *St. Louis Post-Dispatch*, 5 March 1972, 4C.

21. I wish to express my debt to Richard J. Schneider's superb theological critique of *Omensetter's Luck*, "The Fortunate Fall in William Gass's *Omensetter's Luck*," *Critique: Studies in Modern Fiction* 18 (Summer 1976): 5–20.

22. See Michael J. Hoffman, *Gertrude Stein* (Boston: Twayne Publishers, 1976), 5–9.

23. Allegra Stewart in Hoffman, *Gertrude Stein*, 69.

24. Jung, *Aion*, 229.

25. Ibid., 228.

26. Ibid., 229.

Chapter Three

1. Saltzman, *Fiction of William Gass*, 57. This book has been very helpful to me in writing this chapter. I express my debt to Saltzman and recommend this study for a thorough exploration of the basic themes in Gass's fiction.

2. *In the Heart of the Heart of the Country* (New York: Harper & Row, 1968), 32–33; hereafter cited in the text.

3. In an interview, William Gass once stated that "The Pedersen Kid" is the only story that he has written that did not start with the "concrete symbol": it had its "story line first" (quoted in LeClair, *Anything Can Happen*, 168). In an interview with Arthur Saltzman, Gass stated that this story was a turning point in his ideas about language and character; he decided that language should rule the character regardless of verisimilitude (*Fiction of William Gass*, 160).

4. Saltzman, *Fiction of William Gass*, 60–61.

5. Clyde Laurence Hardin, "Wittgenstein on Private Languages," in *Essays on Wittgenstein*, ed. E. D. Klemke (Urbana: University of Illinois Press, 1971), 175.

6. Laurence Perrine, *Sound and Sense: An Introduction to Poetry* (New York: Harcourt, Brace, Jovanovich, 1982), 188.

7. Tom LeClair, *In the Loop: Don DeLillo and the Systems Novel* (Urbana: University of Illinois Press, 1987), 4–5.

8. Saltzman, *Fiction of William Gass*, 89.

9. William Gass, quoted from "A Symposium on Fiction: Donald Barthelme, William Gass, Grace Paley, Walker Percy," *Shenandoah* 7 (Winter 1976): 7.

10. William Butler Yeats, *The Collected Poems of W. B. Yeats* (New York: Macmillan, 1963), 191–92.

11. Frederick Busch, "But This Is What It Is to Live in Hell: William Gass's 'In the Heart of the Heart of the Country,'" *Modern Fiction Studies* 20 (Autumn 1974): 99. I consider this article to be the best written so far on William Gass. It is a succinct statement of all the themes underlying Gass's fiction.

12. Ibid., 100.

13. Ibid.

14. Mircea Eliade, *The Sacred and the Profane: The Nature of Religion* (New York: Harper & Row, 1975), 64–65.

15. Frank Kermode, *The Sense of an Ending* (New York: Oxford University Press, 1967), 44. I am indebted to Kermode's familiar analysis of plot and apocalypse.

16. Eliade, *Sacred and Profane*, 85.

17. Kermode, *The Sense of an Ending*, 44–45.

18. Hippolytus describes one of the *deiknymena* in the mysteries of Eleusis as a lone head of harvested corn or other grain that is held up and adored in silence. This act ritualizes the profound presence of life in the vegetal cycle and, by extension, in all things. Marvin W. Meyer, ed., *The Ancient Mysteries: A Sourcebook* (San Francisco: Harper & Row, 1987), 19.

19. Busch, "But This Is What It Is to Live in Hell," 106.

20. Richard Kostelanetz, "New Fiction in America," in *Surfiction*, 86.

21. Ronald Sukenick, *98.6* (New York: Fiction Collective, 1975), 167.

22. LeClair, *In the Loop*, 11. I am indebted to LeClair for this discussion.

Chapter Four

1. Larry McCaffery, "The Art of Metafiction: William Gass's *Willie Masters' Lonesome Wife*," *Critique* 18 (Summer 1976): 23. I acknowledge my debt to McCaffery for this discussion.

2. Saltzman, *Fiction of William Gass*, 105–6.

3. McCaffery, "Art of Metafiction," 21.

4. Jerome Klinkowitz, "Literary Disruptions: or, What's Become of American Fiction?," in *Surfiction*, 178.

5. See James Schmidt, *Maurice Merleau-Ponty: Between Phenomenology and Structuralism* (New York: St. Martin's Press, 1985), 109.

6. LeClair, *Anything Can Happen*, 158.

7. Ibid.

8. Ibid.

9. McCaffery, "Art of Metafiction," 23.

10. I reiterate here the system that I use to document this unpaginated work (New York: Alfred A. Knopf, 1971). I indicate in parenthesis the section that I cite: (first). The first section (first) ends with the picture of the nude and the caption "00-00-00 . . ."; the second section (second) ends on the page before the appearance of the woman's leg; the third section (third) ends before the first glossy white page that marks the beginning of the fourth section (fourth). I also refer to the color of the paper used in the *Tri-Quarterly* edition.

11. LeClair, *Anything Can Happen*, 158.

12. Ibid.

13. Ibid.

14. McCauley, in *The New Fiction*, 71.

15. Ronald Sukenick, "The New Tradition in Fiction," in *Surfiction*, 38.

16. See McCaffery, "Art of Metafiction," 25, for a succinct discussion of the paper and colors of the book.

17. Federman, "Surfiction," in *Surfiction*, 9–10.

18. McCaffery, "Art of Metafiction," 25–26.

19. *On Being Blue: A Philosophical Inquiry* (Boston: David R. Godine, 1976); hereafter cited in the text as *OBB*.

20. LeClair, *Anything Can Happen*, 158.

21. See Anthony Kenny, *The Legacy of Wittgenstein* (New York: Basil Blackwell, 1984), chapter 6, for a good discussion of private language.

22. McCaffery, "Art of Metafiction," 26–27.

23. Ibid.

24. McCaffery, *Metafictional Muse*, 10–11.

25. Donald Barthelme, *Snow White*, 82–83.

26. Raymond Federman, *Double or Nothing* (Chicago: Swallow Press, 1971), 0.

27. Federman, *Double or Nothing*, 200.

28. Federman, "Surfiction," in *Surfiction*, 13.

29. McCaffery, *Metafictional Muse*, 171.

30. For a clear, readable summary of this portion of the history of philosophy, see Will Durant, *The Story of Philosophy* (New York: Washington Square Press, 1961), chapter 6.

Chapter Five

1. The titular quote of William Gass is from an interview with LeClair in *Anything Can Happen*, 171.

2. LeClair, *Anything Can Happen*, 171.

3. Ibid., 170.

4. Ibid.

5. Saltzman, *Fiction of William Gass*, 117.

6. Ibid.

7. "Why Windows Are Important to Me," *Tri-Quarterly* 20 (Winter 1971): 293–94; hereafter cited in the text as "Windows."

8. LeClair, *Anything Can Happen*, 170.

9. Ibid.

10. Ibid., 170–71.

11. Ibid.

12. Ibid.

13. My title for this section is quoted from Gass's "Life in a Chair," *Salmagundi* 55 (Winter 1982): 6; hereafter cited in the text.

14. "Mad Meg," *Iowa Review* 7 (Winter 1976): 81; hereafter cited in the text as "Mad Meg."

15. LeClair, *Anything Can Happen*, 169.

16. I comment on this series of Fowles's characters based on the magus and its

counterparts in Greek and Egyptian lore of Hermes Trismegistus-Thoth in my article "The Killing of the Weasel: Hermetism in the Fiction of John Fowles," *English Language Notes* 22, no. 3 (March 1985): 69–71.

17. William Gass in an interview with Saltzman, *Fiction of William Gass*, 164.

18. See Max Black's *A Companion to Wittgenstein's "Tractatus"* (Ithaca, N.Y.: Cornell University Press, 1964), 14–15.

19. Gass in an interview with Saltzman, *Fiction of William Gass*, 166.

20. "The Old Folks," *Kenyon Review* 1 (Winter 1979): 38; hereafter cited in the text as "Old Folks."

21. "Susu, I Approach You in My Dreams," *Tri-Quarterly* 42 (Spring 1978): 138; hereafter cited in the text as "Susu."

22. "We Have Not Lived the Right Life," *New American Review* 5 (1969): 4; hereafter cited in the text as "Right Life."

23. "Summer Bees," *Paris Review* 79 (1981): 231; hereafter cited in the text as "Summer Bees."

24. "The Cost of Everything," *Fiction* 1, no. 3 (1972): unpaginated; hereafter cited in the text as "Cost."

25. Elimelech and Naomi, from Bethlehem, take their sons Chilion and Mahlon to another land (Moab) to find a better economic climate (Israel suffers from famine). With time, Elimelech dies, leaving Naomi alone with her sons. When Chilion and Mahlon are grown, they marry Orpah and Ruth respectively. Soon both of Naomi's sons die, and Naomi decides to return to her home where the famine has come to an end and the economy has improved. Orpah stays with her family in Moab; Ruth, leaving her parents, opts to go to Bethlehem with Naomi, even though her mother-in-law advises her against it. In Bethlehem, Ruth works in the fields of Boaz, a wealthy farmer and kinsman of Naomi. Naomi suggests that Ruth sleep at the feet of Boaz and propose marriage to him. Ruth replies, "I will do whatever you say" (Ruth 3:5). Boaz, addressing Ruth as "my child," accepts her, realizing that her proposal is really made out of obedience to Naomi: "Naturally you would prefer a younger man, even though he were poor. But you have put aside your personal desires" (Ruth 3:10).

26. LeClair, *Anything Can Happen*, 154.

Afterword

1. Wilde, *Middle Grounds*, 97.
2. McHale, *Postmodernist Fiction*, 145.

Selected Bibliography

PRIMARY WORKS

Novels

Omensetter's Luck. New York: New American Library, 1966; paperback, Plume Books, 1972.

Willie Masters' Lonesome Wife. Tri-Quarterly Supplement 2. Evanston, Ill.: Northwestern University Press, 1968. New York: Alfred A. Knopf, 1971.

Short Story Collection

In the Heart of the Heart of the Country. New York: Harper & Row, 1968.

Uncollected Short Stories

"The Clairvoyant." *Location* 1–2 (Summer 1964): 59–66.
"The Cost of Everything." *Fiction* 1, no. 3 (1972): unpaginated.
"I Wish You Wouldn't." *Partisan Review* 42, no. 3 (1975): 344–60.
"Koh Whistles Up a Wind." *Tri-Quarterly* 41 (Fall 1977): 191–209.
"Life in a Chair." *Salmagundi* 55 (Winter 1982): 3–60.
"Mad Meg." *Iowa Review* 7 (Winter 1976): 77–95.
"The Old Folks." *Kenyon Review* 1 (Winter 1979): 35–49.
"The Sugar Crock." *Art and Literature* 9 (Summer 1966): 158–71.
"Summer Bees." *Paris Review* 79 (1981).
"Susu, I Approach You in My Dreams." *Tri-Quarterly* 42 (Spring 1978): 122–42.
"Uncle Balt and the Nature of Being." *Conjunctions* 2 (Spring–Summer 1982): 18–29.
"We Have Not Lived the Right Life." *New American Review* 6 (1969): 7–32.
"Why Windows Are Important to Me." *Tri-Quarterly* 20 (Winter 1971): 285–307.

Essay Collections

Fiction and the Figures of Life. New York: Alfred A. Knopf, 1970; paperback, Vintage Books, 1972.

The World within the Word. New York: Alfred A. Knopf, 1978.

Habitations of the Word. New York: Simon & Schuster, 1985.

On Being Blue: A Philosophical Inquiry. Boston: David R. Godine, 1976.

SECONDARY WORKS

Interviews

Duncan, Jeffrey L. "A Conversation with Stanley Elkin and William Gass." *Iowa Review* 7, no. 1 (1976): 48–77.

"A Symposium on Fiction: Donald Barthelme, William Gass, Grace Paley, Walker Percy." *Shenandoah* 7 (Winter 1976): 3–31. Gass is challenged about his theories of fiction by other well-known modern writers.

Books

Alter, Robert. *Partial Magic: The Novel As a Self-conscious Genre.* Berkeley and Los Angeles: University of California Press, 1975. Excellent background reading on the history of self-conscious or metafictional prose from Cervantes to the contemporaries of William Gass.

Saltzman, Arthur M. *The Fiction of William Gass: The Consolation of Language.* Crosscurrents: Modern Critiques, 3d series. Edited by Jerome Klinkowitz. Carbondale and Edwardsville, Ill.: Southern Illinois University Press, 1986. A solid general introduction to William Gass's principal works. Includes an interview.

Articles and Parts of Books

Allen, Carolyn J. "Fiction and Figures of Life in *Omensetter's Luck.*" *Pacific Coast Philology* 9 (1974): 5–11. A discussion of theory and practice in Gass's novel.

Bassoff, Bruce. "The Sacrificial World of William Gass: *In the Heart of the Heart of the Country.*" *Critique: Studies in Modern Fiction* 18 (August 1976): 36–42. Some interesting insights into the stories. Stretched a bit at times to fit Bassoff's thesis.

Busch, Frederick. "But This Is What It Is to Live in Hell: William Gass's 'In the Heart of the Heart of the Country.'" *Modern Fiction Studies* 20 (Autumn 1974): 328–36. An insightful and penetrating study. I consider this to be the best critical article on Gass's work.

Crinklaw, Don. "It's All a Matter of Style." St. Louis *Post-Dispatch* (5 March 1972), 4C. Interesting comments about Gass's life in St. Louis; also good interview material.

Donoghue, Denis. *Ferocious Alphabets.* Boston: Little, Brown, 1981. Negative criticism of Gass as an "exhibitionist" on occasion.

French, Ned. "Against the Grain: Theory and Practice in the Work of William H. Gass." *Iowa Review* 7 (Winter 1976): 96–106. French contends that fortunately Gass does not follow his own theory in his fiction writing.

Gilman, Richard. "William H. Gass." In *The Confusion of Realms.* New York:

Random House/Vintage, 1969. Worthwhile general assessment of Gass's early work.

Kane, Patricia. "The Sun Burned on the Snow: Gass's 'The Pedersen Kid.'" *Critique* 14, no. 2 (December 1972): 89–96. Excellent explanation of the central metaphor and the action of Gass's most commented-upon story.

LeClair, Thomas. *Anything Can Happen: Interviews with Contemporary American Novelists.* Urbana, Ill.: University of Illinois Press, 1983. The interview with Gass is the best so far. LeClair leads Gass into an excellent self-portrait. There is also a version of the Gardner-Gass debate.

McCaffery, Larry. *The Metafictional Muse: The Works of Robert Coover, Donald Barthelme, and William H. Gass.* Pittsburgh: University of Pittsburgh Press, 1982. An indispensable discussion of Gass and metafiction. It is clear and complete.

————. "The Art of Metafiction: William Gass's *Willie Masters' Lonesome Wife.* *Critique* 18 (Summer 1976): 21–35.

McCauley, Carole Spearin. "William Gass: Fiction as World Event." *Ann Arbor Review* 8–9 (Spring 1970): 43–47. Good general discussion of Gass's technique in metaphorizing.

McHale, Brian. *Postmodernist Fiction.* New York: Methuen, 1987. Clear and straightforward. The best treatment of Gass and his generation. Excellent discussion of postmodernist allegory and oppositional elements in metaphor.

Mullinax, Gary. "An Interview with William Gass." *Delaware Literary Magazine* 1 (1972): 81–87. Short and not deep, this interview contains, nevertheless, a few pertinent statements by Gass about his work and theories.

Rodrigues, Eusebio L. "A Nymph at Her Orisons: An Analysis of William Gass's 'Order of Insects.'" *Studies in Short Fiction* 17 (Summer 1980): 348–51. A compact and lucid interpretation of Gass's story as a fictional rendering of Plato's dictum that perception for human beings is a category of pain.

Sanford, Robert. "Socrates Lives." *St. Louis Post-Dispatch* (3 June 1973). Interesting biographical material.

Schneider, Richard J. "The Fortunate Fall in William Gass's *Omensetter's Luck.*" *Critique: Studies in Modern Fiction* 18 (Summer 1976): 5–20. Superb study of the Garden archetype in Gass's novel.

Scholes, Robert. "Metafiction." *Iowa Review 1* (Fall 1970): 100–115. Seminal essay on the literary background and concerns of Gass and his contemporaries.

Tanner, Tony. *City of Words.* London: Trinity Press, 1971. Excellent background source for Gass and his literary generation.

Wilde, Alan. *Middle Grounds: Studies in Contemporary American Fiction.* Philadelphia: University of Pennsylvania Press, 1987. Original and intriguing assessment of Gass and other writers who have been called self-referential or nonrealist.

Bibliography

French, Ned. "William Gass Bibliography." *Iowa Review* 7 (Winter 1976):
     106–7. Good listing of early Gass primary and secondary material.
     Needs updating.

Index